Joe 1

Does It Make Any Difference What I Do ?

MILDRED TENGBOM

BETHANY HOUSE PUBLISHERS
MINNEAPOLIS, MINNESOTA 55438
A Division of Bethany Fellowship, Inc.

Photos by Jon Dugan and Dick Easterday

Scripture quotations are taken from The New American Standard Bible, The Living Bible, The Revised Standard Version, The New International Version, and the Williams Translation, and are marked accordingly. Used by permission.

Published by Bethany House Publishers
A Division of Bethany Fellowship, Inc.
6820 Auto Club Road, Minneapolis, MN 55438

Printed in the United States of America

Library of Congress Cataloging in Publication Data

Tengbom, Mildred.
    Does it make any difference what I do?

    Summary: Anecdotes highlighting a variety of problems faced by young people in their daily lives are followed by discussion questions and an appropriate Biblical verse.
    1. Youth—Conduct of life. 2. Youth—Religious life.
[1. Conduct of life. 2. Christian life] I. Title.
BJ1661.T45   1984   241   84-14486
ISBN 0-87123-448-3

The Author

MILDRED TENGBOM was born in Minnesota, and at an early age developed a passion for reading and writing. At age 15 Christ became real to her, and she eventually went to the borders of Nepal as a missionary. After her marriage to Dr. Tengbom, she served again as a missionary—this time in East Africa. The Tengboms have two sons and two daughters, all followers of Christ.

Mrs. Tengbom has written several books. Her work has been published in over fifty secular and religious periodicals. She is listed in *Personalities of the West and Midwest, Contemporary Authors and International Writers* and *Authors' Who's Who*. Her articles on the POW/MIA issue are included in the *Congressional Records*, and her biography on Clara Maass has received recognition by the Army Nurses Corps and is in their libraries.

Books by Mildred Tengbom

Is Your God Big Enough?
The Bonus Years
Table Prayers
Fill My Cup, Lord (with Dr. Luverne C. Tengbom)
Bible Readings for Families (with Dr. Luverne C. Tengbom)
No Greater Love: The Story of Clara Maass
Sometimes I Hurt
Help for Bereaved Parents
Help for Families of the Terminally Ill
Devotions for New Mothers
Especially for Mother
Mealtime Prayers
Why Waste Your Illness? Let God Use It for Growth
Does Anyone Care How I Feel?
I Wish I Felt Good All the Time

Hi Kids,

Who of us doesn't want friends? We all want at least one or two—someone with whom we can talk and tell all the things that trouble us, as well as share happy times—don't we?

Our parents can be some of our best friends. The trouble is, sometimes it's hard to know how to get started talking with our parents about things we really would like to discuss. *Does It Make Any Difference What I Do?* was written to help you do just that.

You can use this book whenever you feel a need to talk about something special referred to in the book. Maybe you are wondering how to get over feeling jealous of your sister. Or you find yourself spending most of the time thinking about boys and want to know what to do about it. Or you may be confused about any number of other things: parents getting a divorce, video games, pressure to win in sports. Kids have lots of problems.

You may want to ask your parents to set aside some time one night a week when you can talk. Reading a portion from this book together will help you discuss things that are important to you.

You also may enjoy reading this book with some of your friends and discussing the questions. As you do so, you will be sorting out your values. You will begin to understand which things are most important to you and why. You'll feel better when you get these things straightened out, and you'll feel stronger and more courageous to stand up for what you believe.

God bless you! He loves you more than you could ever understand.

Contents

A Word to Parents and Teachers

As parents and teachers, one of our chief concerns is to know what we can do to help our children adopt biblical, moral, and spiritual values which will guide them through life and give them a sense of stability and security.

We recognize the importance of modeling those values in our own lives. For example, we can't say to our child, "Don't smoke. It's harmful to your health," and then smoke.

But, can we do more than model? Is there some way we also can teach? The answer is yes!

Lasting, trustworthy and authentic values are not learned only by seeing values modeled. They are also learned by reasoning, and parents and teachers can guide children in their reasoning.

To do so, parents and teachers need to understand in what ways children of different ages reason. Seven to eleven-year-olds understand what parents consider right or wrong by the method of punishment or reward. These children then begin to realize that other people have rights too, and must learn how to live with others.

The preadolescents and young adolescents, for whom this book is written, put great value on the judgment and opinion of others who are significant in their lives. These people can be peers, teachers, parents or members of their particular "in" group. They also are beginning to attach importance to the values society in general upholds. As young people grow older they need to be led a step further: to consider what values society *ought* to uphold.

Growth occurs only as we are challenged to stretch beyond what we already know. Consequently, even young adolescents need to be challenged to think about what values society *ought* to embrace in contrast to the ones they already do.

In other words, growth occurs as we move from one stage to another.

Stage One: What do *I* think is important?

Stage Two: What do *others* think is important?

Stage Three: What *ought* to be important?

A child in Stage One obeys because obedience will bring rewards and disobedience, punishment. Obedience is forced. In Stage Two, the child chooses to obey because others expect him or her to do so. In Stage Three, the child obeys because he or she *wants* to obey, out of love for the one from whom obedience is asked.

Growth varies for all of us throughout our entire lives. We may be able to make progress in one area and lag in another. So too with children. As parents frequently talk with and listen to their children, asking questions that will cause the children to think, they can help them pass from one stage to another. It is especially needful to help children and young people recognize that what they do affects others (and why it affects others).

The atmosphere in which this conscious teaching takes place is supremely important. A time to talk should be decided on ahead of time so it can be unhurried. The parents or teachers and young people should both agree to give reasonable time to each discussion, usually from twenty minutes to half an hour.

The atmosphere also should be pleasant and loving. One of the best times for many parents is after an evening meal. Eating relaxes and cheers us up, usually putting us in good moods.

Above all, teaching should not come immediately after a conflict or period of tension between parents or teachers and young people.

Eight general values are explored in this book:

1. *Respect.* This will include courtesy, recognition, honor, admiration, and compliments.

2. *Power.* By this we mean the part youth play in making important decisions. Decision-making involves power. How we use the power we have reflects and determines our character. We shall consider leadership, influence, authority and decision-making.

3. *Wealth.* We shall consider goods, money, income, property, food, shelter, clothing, and performing a service.

4. *Enlightenment.* That is, knowledge, education, learning,

understanding, information. Why are these important? How do they affect us?

5. *Skill*. We shall think of motor skills, thinking skills, communication skills, social skills, and aesthetic skills.

6. *Well-being*. A loss of well-being may cause a loss of status in other respects. We shall consider the importance of health, happiness, feeling well, contentment, relaxation, being at peace with God and people.

7. *Integrity*. This will include ethical decisions. We shall consider honesty, fair play, justice, responsibility, trust, keeping one's promises.

8. *Affection*. We shall consider the love, fondness and friendship we feel toward our families and friends. We also shall consider the loyalty we feel to a group, country or state. And most importantly, we shall consider our relationship to God.

We understand, of course, that being able to think through and give the right answers is only one step. Values recognized as being biblical and authentic need to be woven into one's life. This takes a lifetime. But identifying the values and acknowledging their worth is a process that can and should take place in the home before the child leaves home. If the child comes from a home where parents are disinterested, then Christian teachers can fill this role. This book is designed to help parents and teachers with that task.

As with previous books for younger children, I suggest that the young person reads the portion and leads in asking the questions. As discussion follows, you as parents and teachers need to be sensitive to the reactions of your young people. If you note puzzled expressions suggesting disagreement say, "Maybe you see it differently. Tell me how you see it." It takes imagination and effort to see things as children see them, but it is not impossible. And only as this is done is it possible for parents and teachers and young people to have loving and respectful communication.

1

I Was Trying So Hard to Be Number One

I'm so happy, Lord, I could cry.
I *am* crying.
For a whole year I've been practicing swimming—
    hours every day.
I thought if I could win in the state tournament,
    maybe Mom and Dad
    would like me as much as they like Julie.
I've always wished I was smart like Julie.
She's pretty too,
    and slim,
    and popular.
It's seemed to me that
    Dad was always teasing Julie,
    and Mom was always buying her new clothes,
    and I've been feeling
        that they didn't care much about me at all.
Anyway, I've been trying so hard to be number one
    in swimming.
    I thought they would pay more attention to me then.
I was trying so hard.
Tonight I came home from swimming practice
    and threw myself on the bed
    and cried and cried.
I was so sick of swimming!
I ache all over,
    and with all this practice,
    I haven't had any time for my friends.
Mom came in and sat down on the floor
    beside my bed
    and started to rub my back.

"I hate swimming!" I exploded.
Mom's hand stopped rubbing my back for a minute
    but then started again.
"You hate swimming," she repeated,
    but her voice sounded a little bewildered.
"I hate it!" I screamed.
    "I wouldn't do it another day if I didn't . . ."
Mom waited.
"If what?" she asked.
"If I didn't think maybe you'd love me more if I won the
    tournament."
My words came out all in a rush.
The back-rubbing faltered.
Then I felt something wet on the back of my neck.
I rolled over.
Mom was crying.
"We never knew you felt that way, Stacey," she said.
"I'm so, so sorry."
She was quiet for a minute.
"We love you very much, Stacey," she said. "Just as you are.
You don't have to be number one in *anything*
    just to please us.
    Oh, Stacey, I'm *so* sorry!"
That's why *I'm* crying, Lord.
It's such a relief to know Mom and Dad do love me—
    just like I am.

Let's Think and Talk

1. Parents' love for each of their children may show itself in distinct ways. They may have different feelings toward each child. But does this mean they don't love all their children? Talk about this aspect of parental love. Ask parents to explain their unique feelings of love for each of their children and what makes each of their kids special to them. Ask them how this was true for them in the way their parents loved them.

2. Stacey thought *doing* was more important than *being*. Which do you think is the more important and why?

3. What lack in their family life does the misunderstanding between Stacey and her parents reveal?

4. How could they avoid this kind of misunderstanding in the future?

5. What do you think your parents do not understand about you?

6. Can we "win" love? Discuss this.

A Verse to Remember

"Love never fails" (1 Cor. 13:8, NASB).

2

I've Got to Lose Some Weight!

I just about died, Lord.
I stepped on Mom's scale today—
    I've gained five pounds,
    and I haven't grown an inch!
I stood on a chair
    and turned this way and that
    and looked in the mirror,
    but I hadn't grown out where I want to grow out,
    so I got really worried.
I guessed it must be all that lasagna and chocolate cake
    and pancakes and hot chocolate
    and mocha ice cream.
I decided right there and then,
    I'm gonna diet.
If I tried real hard,
    maybe I could get real skinny—
    like Laura Jenkins.
Maybe Peter would talk to me then.
I didn't eat anything the rest of the day.
Mom wasn't home,
    and Dad didn't notice,
    so that was easy.
This morning I skipped off to school
    before Mom could say anything.
But by supper I had a headache,
    so I ate to get rid of it.
Then I went upstairs
    and stuck my finger down my throat
    like they say Laura Jenkins does to stay skinny,
    but I guess my fingers are too short and stubby

so they didn't go down far enough.
I just gagged,
    but that was all.
So I don't know.
Maybe I won't be able to be skinny
    like Laura Jenkins after all.
I wonder if Peter will talk to me
    even if I'm not skinny.

Let's Think and Talk

1. Do you know any girls like Laura Jenkins?
2. Why do they diet so severely?
3. What can happen to our bodies when we don't eat properly?
4. How can we tell if we are too skinny or too fat?
5. Why do people overeat?
6. How should you change your eating habits (what kind of food, how much)?

Verses to Remember

"Give your bodies to God. Let them be a living sacrifice, holy—the kind he can accept. When you think of what he has done for you, is this too much to ask? Don't copy the behavior and customs of this world, but be a new and different person with a fresh newness in all you do and think" (Rom. 12:1, 2, TLB).

3

But I Like Judy Blume's Books!

Myrna and Chuck and Lois and Kathy
   came over last night.
We're all working together on an English assignment.
We hadn't intended to,
   but we got into the biggest argument.
We started talking about what books we liked.
Lois said she liked *A Wrinkle in Time*.
Chuck liked *Then Again, Maybe I Won't*.
Lois asked him,
   "You like *that* book?"
"Why not?" Chuck sparked defensively.
"I don't like a hero
   who goes spying with binoculars, looking at girls dressing,"
   Lois said.
"That wasn't the only thing in the story," Chuck argued.
"No, Tony got rich and liked it," Lois said.
"What's wrong with that?" Chuck asked.
"It's wrong if it turns Tony into a window-peeper," Lois
   retorted.
"Quit arguing, you two," Kathy pleaded.
   "So what, if you think Judy Blume blew it with that book?
   She's written other good books."
"Like?" Lois said.
"*Are You There, God? It's Me, Margaret*," answered Kathy.
"The teacher in our school said
   she wouldn't give us credit
   for reading that one," Lois said.
"My mom didn't like it when she saw me reading it," piped
   Myrna.

About then I thought I might as well
　　join the argument.
"So what's wrong with that book?" I asked.
　　"I like Judy Blume's books.
　　They're not goody-goody."
　　They're real, but not too real."
"My teacher asked how anyone could say to God,
　　like Margaret did in her prayer, 'Haven't I always done what
　　you wanted?' " Myrna said.
"She was just trying to get to know God," I said.
　　"She had to do it all by herself.
　　Her parents weren't helping her."
"She wished they would," Kathy said.
　　"She thought deciding what religion one should follow is
　　hard when you're twelve,
　　that twelve is too late to learn;
　　and if she had any children,
　　she would tell them what religion they were,
　　so they could start learning about it early."
"My mom didn't like the way the book
　　made fun of church and priests and ministers," Myrna said.
"They maybe seem kinda strange
　　if you haven't grown up used to them," I tried to explain.
　　"They do dress differently.
　　Margaret was just trying to make connection with God
　　because she had this problem."
"What problem?" Chuck said.
　　"I dunno what you're talking about.
　　I haven't read the book."
We girls looked at each other.
How could we tell Chuck
　　that Margaret's biggest problem was
　　too personal to talk about
　　with boys?
I felt my cheeks getting warm
　　just thinking about discussing the subject in front of a boy.
"She never did find God, did she?" Myrna asked.
"Well, not like we do in church," I said.
　　"But she was still talking to God by the end of the book,
　　so I can't help but feel
　　He wouldn't let her down then, would He,

when she wanted to know Him?"

"But you can't know God just right out of the air," Myrna argued.

"He just doesn't drop down on you."

"Let's get on with our assignment," Chuck said.

"I've got to go to basketball practice pretty quick."

So that's where we left Margaret, Lord.

I hope you find her.

Let's Think and Talk

1. What books do you like to read?
2. How do you feel about books with profanity?
3. What books have you read that left you feeling down?
4. What books have you read that left you feeling hopeful?
5. What morals are portrayed in the books you have read? Which ones are in harmony with what God's Word teaches us, and which aren't?
6. In what ways do books influence us?
7. Do your parents know what books you are reading? Do you want them to know?

A Verse to Remember

"Whatever is true, whatever is honorable, whatever is right, whatever is pure, whatever is lovely, whatever is of good repute, if there is any excellence and if anything worthy of praise, let your mind dwell on these things" (Phil. 4:8, NASB).

4

Who Needs a Different Outfit Every Day?

Schools are sure different.
Last year our family lived back East
    and I went to a private school.
Clothes there were terribly important.
If you wore preppy clothes,
    you were "in."

If you didn't,
    you were "out,"
    and I mean *really* out.
Then we moved.
This year at my new school
    clothes aren't that important.
Last year at that other school
    we felt like we had to wear a different outfit every day.
Here we wouldn't dare do that.
The other kids would think
    we were showing off.
Most of the kids here wear jeans and plain tops.
Some of the girls wear dresses.
If you wear a dress,
    it should be pressed and clean,
    but that's all.
Dad says that the economy has hit this town pretty hard,
    and maybe that's one of the reasons
    clothes aren't as important here
    as they were in that private school last year.
To be "in" here you have to be
    a caring person,
    active in sports or chorus
    or student council
    or something.
It's sure different.
I think I like this school better,
    even if I miss my old friends.

Let's Think and Talk

1. What is important in your school?
2. When the emphasis is on clothes, what particular group of boys and girls suffers?
3. What do you think about dress codes for schools?
4. What is important to you when you choose friends?
5. How would you solve this situation? Maria is a new girl at a school where clothes are important. Both Maria's mother and father work, but there are many children in the family. Maria is a good student. She sings well, and she wants friends.

But Maria's parents cannot afford to buy Maria many clothes. What can Maria do?

A Verse to Remember

"Don't be concerned about the outward beauty that depends on jewelry, or beautiful clothes, or hair arrangement. Be beautiful inside, in your hearts, with the lasting charm of a gentle and quiet spirit which is so precious to God" (1 Pet. 3:4, TLB).

5

How Can I Help Laurie?

Dear God,
I'm worried about Laurie.
I think her mother beats her.
To begin with, I used to wonder
    why she always wore tops with long sleeves.
But then when I got a locker next to hers
    and we undressed for P.E.
    I understood.
She always had black and blue marks on her arms.
"I bruise real easily," she said.
I thought maybe she was one of those—
    what do they call them?—bleeders.
Then one day she came to school with a black eye.
"I ran into a door in the dark," she said.
Yesterday she was absent,
    and I offered to take her homework to her.
She was lying on the davenport,
    and her arm was in a sling.
"I'm always having accidents," she said,
    but then she began to cry.
I don't know what to do.
How can I help her, Lord?

Let's Think and Talk

1. What could you do to help Laurie?
2. Do you know anyone who is being beaten or abused?
3. Why do children like Laurie often hesitate to ask for help?
4. Why do some parents beat their children?

24

5. What does it do to a child when he or she is constantly mistreated? How is his personality affected?

6. How can parents be helped so they won't mistreat their children?

A Verse to Remember

"Fathers, do not provoke your children to anger, but bring them up in the discipline and instruction of the Lord" (Eph. 6:4, RSV).

6

Dad Thought He'd Manage on His Own

Mom and Dad had never been able to understand
  why some people are poor.
"They're lazy," Dad used to say.
  "In North America, you can always earn a living if you
  want to.
But now it's happened to us.
Dad's been out of work for a year,
  and yesterday Mom was laid off.
It looked like we might have to sell our home and move—
  but Dad didn't know if we would be able to sell it.
Then last night Mr. Simeon, Dad's former boss, came,
  and Dad and he talked behind closed doors for a long time.
Afterward, Dad said Mr. Simeon had offered
  to loan him some money at no interest
  until Dad or Mom can get work again
  and make the mortgage payments.
I guess the thing that surprised me most
  was that Dad said he'd sure be happy for the loan.
Dad told Mom he never knew people could care so much
  and be so kind,
  and then he blew his nose real hard.

Let's Think and Talk

1. Why do some people find it difficult to receive help?
2. What examples of pride and false pride do we see here?
3. If Dad had refused help, what would it have meant for his family?

4. Have you ever had a hard time accepting help? Have your parents? Tell about it.

5. How can we offer people help in a way that will make it easier for them to accept?

6. Do you know anybody who is unemployed and is having trouble making ends meet?

7. What could you do to help?

Verses to Remember

"Of course, I don't mean that those who receive your gifts should have an easy time of it at your expense, but you should divide with them. Right now you have plenty and can help them; then at some other time they can share with you when you need it. In this way each will have as much as he needs. Do you remember what the Scriptures say about this? 'He that gathered much had nothing left over, and he that gathered little had enough.' So you also should share with those in need" (2 Cor. 8:13–15, TLB).

7

What's Happened to Granny?

Dear God,
Are you there?
I'm hurting really bad.
I can't understand what has happened to Granny.
    Granny was always so interested in what was going on at
        school.
    Granny used to have time to listen to me.
    Granny always seemed to understand what I was going
        through.
    Granny made such fantastic meals and baked my favorite
        chocolate angel food cake.
    This Granny, my Granny, just isn't Granny anymore.
I remember when she started complaining
    that she couldn't remember things.
Then she started doing strange things,
    such as leaving the stove on all night
    or burning the cake in the oven.
And then one day I came home
    and found her in the backyard
    dressed in just her underwear!
I was so glad she was in the *back*yard.
When I took her by the hand to lead her in,
    she became real stubborn
    and didn't want to go.
The next day she wandered down the street
    in her nightgown.
After that, Mom and Dad knew they had to make a decision.
With both Mom and Dad working,
    it just wasn't safe to leave Granny alone at home anymore.

And with us kids going to private schools,
    Mom has to work.
We were fortunate to have a nice care home
    right here in our town,
    and they had a room for Granny.
I go to see her every Saturday, Lord.
She's dressed nicely,
    and her hair is curled;
    but she's tied in her chair,
    and she doesn't even know me.
Half the time I can't even understand
    what she's saying.
She calls me Sybil instead of Joy—
    Mom says Sybil was Granny's little sister.
She's so thin, and I can see right through her skin.
I feel like I've lost my Granny.
I can't understand what has happened,
    and I worry:
        will it happen to Mom?
        will it happen to me when I get old?

Let's Think and Talk

1. Do you know anyone like Joy's grandmother?

2. How would finding out more about Granny's problems help Joy?

3. What alternative did Joy's parents have to finding a care home for Granny? If you were making the decision, what choice would you make?

4. How can Joy continue to show her love and affection for Granny?

5. Is there any point in continuing to visit Granny when she doesn't seem to know anybody? Talk about this.

A Verse to Remember

"This is pure and undefiled religion in the sight of our God and Father, to visit orphans and widows in their distress" (James 1:27, NASB).

8

I Love My Cat

I don't know what I'd do without Thai, Lord.
Thai's our cat, you know.
We named her Thai
    because she's Siamese,
    and Siamese cats came from Thailand, didn't they?
My mom's not too happy with cats in the house,
    but she makes allowances for Thai
    because she thinks Thai is a beautiful cat,
    and because Thai's neutered
    and has had her claws removed.
Otherwise she wouldn't let us keep her.
Now Dad's different.
He *loves* Thai.
He's taught her how to somersault
    when he throws her in the air.
He puts her on the seat of the high-backed overstuffed chair
    in the living room—the gold one—
    and then he squats on the floor behind the chair
    and reaches up and peers over the edge.
When Thai jumps for him,
    Dad pulls his head down
    and disappears out of Thai's sight
    and laughs.
Dad gets really silly with Thai;
    I'm glad he likes her.
I think cats need to be liked.
It's my job to rinse out Thai's bowl and give her fresh water
    and see that she has enough dry food.
Once in a while, for a treat, we give her canned food.
I don't like opening canned cat food.
    It really stinks, and I have to hold my nose.

I have to empty the kitty litter box too.
Sometimes that stinks something awful.
    and I just about vomit,
    but then I think,
    if you love someone like I love Thai,
    it helps you overlook those disgusting chores.
And when Thai rubs against my leg and mews,
    or is waiting at the door for me to come home,
    or hops up on my bed and snuggles close, I know it's all worth it.
Honestly, Lord, I don't know what I'd do without my cat.

Let's Think and Talk

1. What character traits in Linda were developed because she had Thai?

2. Do you have a pet?

3. What does having a pet teach you?

4. Did your parents ever have pets? Ask them to tell you about their pets.

Verses to Remember

The Bible doesn't have much to say about pets, but there is a reference to a pet in 2 Samuel 12:1–25. You may want to read this portion. Verses 1–3 are:

"There were two men in a certain city, one very rich . . . and the other very poor, owning nothing but a little lamb he had managed to buy. It was his children's pet and he fed it from his own plate and let it drink from his own cup; he cuddled it in his arms like a baby daughter" (TLB).

9

Mom Surprised Me

I was mistaken, Lord.
I thought Mom didn't really care too much about Thai,
    but just endured her
    for our sake.
Now I realize I didn't know
    how she felt.
You see, Lord, something awfully sad has happened.
Thai is dead.
She'd been sick for weeks,
    so Mom and Dad took her to a vet.
He examined her and shook his head.
"Old age," he said.
    "There are so many things wrong with her
    there's no way we could fix everything."
I couldn't believe it!
Mom and Dad wanted to put Thai to sleep,
    but I said, "No way!
    Thai's not going to die! She can't!"
I took my allowance money
    and bought her canned food
    and tuna
    so she could have some every day,
    but she just left it in the dish.
She didn't even want to lick my fingers
    when I put whipped cream on them
    especially for her.
I knew then that she really was sick.
But still I kept hoping she'd get well.
Today I came home from school
    and Mom was all red-eyed.
"Thai's dead," she said,
    and showed me the box

where she had laid Thai on a little pillow.
I felt Thai,
  and she was all stiff and cold.
"It's been a terrible day," Mom said,
  starting to cry.
  "I was cleaning the house,
  but Thai didn't want to be alone,
  so she followed me, her legs spread far apart,
  hardly able to walk.
  At last she couldn't walk,
  so she just lay down and lifted her head and mewed so sadly.
"I picked her up," Mom continued,
  "and held her
  and then she was quiet."
Mom blew her nose.
"That's all," she said.
  "She just quit breathing."
Mom walked to the kitchen to get another tissue.
I stood staring at Thai in the little box.
Mom came back.
"I feel so silly," she said,
  her voice getting firm for a minute,
  but then it got shaky again. "I never knew I could get so
  fond of a cat.
"I don't think I ever want a cat again," she said.
  "It's too hard to see it die."
I couldn't believe it, Lord!
I was so surprised at Mom
  that it wasn't until the next day
  that I knew how really sad I was that Thai had died.

Let's Think and Talk

1. Why had Linda not understood how her mother felt about Thai?

2. Why wouldn't Linda give her parents permission to put Thai to sleep?

3. Do people have a similar experience when a person they love is very sick? Why?

4. How did Linda's mother show that she cared about Thai?

5. Have you ever had a pet that died? How did you feel?

6. Did your parents ever have this experience? Talk about this.

7. Linda's mother didn't let others know how fond she was of Thai. Sometimes people behave this way toward each other. They don't tell other people how much they really love them. What happens when people do this?

Verses to Remember

The Apostle Paul expressed to the Christians at Philippi how he felt about them. Note the remarks he made in the letter he wrote to them.

"I have you in my heart" (Phil. 1:7, NASB).

"God is my witness, how I long for you all with the affection of Christ Jesus" (Phil. 1:8, NASB).

"Therefore, my beloved brethren whom I long to see, my joy and crown, so stand firm in the Lord, my beloved" (Phil. 4:1, NASB).

10

Mom and Dad Are Getting a Divorce

Dear God,
I never thought it would happen to *our* family.
Sure, Mom and Dad have disagreements
    and talk loudly sometimes,
        but I never dreamed they didn't love each other anymore
        or would ever think of divorce.
Not *my* parents, Lord.
I knew things were really bad
    when Mom said she wasn't going to the women's conference.
She loves to go to the women's conference.
Every year she and about fifteen other women from church go.
She went to see her friend, Mrs. Stone, to tell her,
    and when she came home
    her eyes were all red.
She hadn't been home long
    before the phone rang,
    and another of her friends was calling.
I listened in on the upstairs phone.
I wanted to find out what really was going on.
"Do you have a lawyer?" her friend asked.
    "And how are you fixed financially?
    Do you have any money?"
I hadn't even thought about that!
Does Mom have any money?
I don't think so.
At least not stashed away.
Dad does all the bank work.
How'll we eat if Mom doesn't have money?
We *will* live with Mom, won't we?
Don't kids usually live with their mothers?

But I don't want to live with Mom if Dad can't live with us, too.
Why is this happening, Lord?
Are we kids to blame?
I know that Mom and Dad haven't always agreed on
    what we should be allowed to do or not do,
    or what school we should attend,
    and sometimes we kids have played one of them against the
    other in order to get our way,
    but don't all kids do that sometimes?
Lord, I don't ever want to get married!

Let's Think and Talk

1. Why do parents get divorced?
2. What alternatives are there to divorce?
3. Who is to blame when parents get divorced?
4. What is difficult for children when parents get divorced?
5. What is difficult for parents when they get divorced?
6. How can a family survive a divorce?
7. Do you know anyone who seems to have survived a divorce quite well? Talk to them if you can.
8. Someday you will very likely be getting married. What can you do, both before you get married and afterward, to prevent a divorce?

Verses to Remember

"The Lord is my helper, I will not be afraid; what can man do to me?" (Heb. 13:6, RSV).

"God is our refuge and strength, a very present help in trouble" (Ps. 46:1, RSV).

11

_____

They Said the Lord Told Them

Dad's been out of work for months.
He doesn't get any checks from the state anymore.
Mom is working,
    but her checks aren't as big as Dad's used to be.

This month was bad.
The dishwasher broke.
    We didn't fix it.
The water softener conked out, too.
    We didn't fix that either.
Jim had to go to the dentist.
    We paid that bill.
My shoes got too tight.
    We found some on sale.
    They weren't ones I really liked,
    but they fit,
    and Mom said that was the most important.
Then the transmission in the car went
    (whatever that means, I'm not sure),
    but Dad said we had to fix the car
    because he needs it to take Mom to work.
He paid the garage man half
    and promised he'd pay the rest next month.
It's a good thing the garage man has known Dad
    for a long time
    and knows he always pays.
Anyway, today after school
    Dad asked if I wanted to go shopping with him.
Mom had made out a long list.
We were going up and down the aisles,
    and I was drawing lines through the items we found,
    when suddenly Dad said, "That's all, Muffin."
"That's all?" I asked.
    "We've got all these things left to get."
I showed him the list.
Dad punched some more buttons on his calculator.
"No, Muffin," he said, "that's all."
And then I began to understand.
After we loaded the bags in the car,
    Dad took my chin in his hand
    and tipped my head back and said, "Muffin, we're not going
    to worry. God has promised to take care of us, and we're just
    going to trust Him."
I wondered what he meant.
What did he think would happen?
We'd been home about an hour

when we heard a car door slam outside.
I thought Mom had gotten a ride home from work,
    but instead the doorbell rang,
    and when Dad opened it,
        there stood three of the ladies from church, each with two
        big grocery bags.
They were laughing.
"The Lord told us to bring these to you," they said.
How had He done that? I wondered.
I knew they were ordinary people like Dad and me.
They weren't Marys or Elizabeths of the Bible.
How did the Lord tell *them*?
He'd never told me to buy groceries for someone.
I can't even get Him to tell me which one of the boys
    is going to like me for sure.
Goodness knows, I've asked Him.
Anyway, it didn't seem to bother Dad
    that the ladies said
    the Lord had told them to bring us groceries.
He just said, "Praise the Lord!"
    and, "Come in, come in!
    This is wonderful!"
And then he told them,
    "When I was checking out our groceries at the supermarket,
    and knew we didn't have enough for the week, I said,
    'Lord, you'll just have to take care of us.' "
I was busy digging the groceries out of the bag,
    but out of the corner of my eye
    I saw Dad brush his cheek with the back of his hand,
    and one of the ladies reached over and hugged him.

Let's Think and Talk

1. What do you think the ladies meant when they said, "The Lord told us"?

2. Have you ever felt the Lord had told you to do something? Tell about it.

3. Why did Lynn's father not find it difficult to accept the ladies' gifts?

4. Read Matthew 6:33 and Philippians 4:19. Has your fam-

ily ever experienced God's supplying certain, specific needs? Talk about this.

5. "The Lord is my shepherd, I have everything I need" (Ps. 23:1, TLB). Yet about 50 million Christians today are so poor they do not get sufficient food nor do they have safe water to drink. What has prevented God from supplying their needs?

A Verse to Remember

"And God is able to make all grace abound toward you; that ye, always having all sufficiency in all things, may abound to every good work" (2 Cor. 9:8, RSV).

12

I Hate It When They Tell <u>My</u> Secrets!

I knew I shouldn't have told Stephanie
    that when I was eight
    I used to boast to my friends
    that I had wings in my drawer at home,
    and if I put them on
    I could jump off that branch 'way up in the big oak tree in
    our schoolyard
    and my wings would hold me up.
I maybe believed it then,
    but I was only eight then,
    and I'm twelve now,
    and you don't believe silly things like that
    when you're twelve.
Anyway, I shouldn't have told Stephanie,
    because she told Jane,
    and Jane told Rebecca,
    and Rebecca—the crumb!—told Peter,
    and they're all laughing.
Every time I pass Peter now
    he holds his hands up by his shoulders
    and wiggles them like wings and laughs.
I hate Peter!
Only I like him too,
    and that's why I hate him!
And I hate Stephanie and Jane and Rebecca even more!

Let's Think and Talk

1. What did Pam feel she had lost because Stephanie broke

her promise and told Pam's secret?

    2. Has anyone ever broken a promise and told your secrets? How did you feel? Talk about this.

    3. Why is being trustworthy important in friendship?

    4. How do parents show their trust in each other?

    5. How do parents show their trust in their children?

    6. How could Pam both hate and like Peter?

    7. When is having a good imagination valuable? Discuss this.

A Verse to Remember

    "He who goes about as a talebearer reveals secrets, but he who is trustworthy conceals a matter" (Prov. 11:13, NASB).

13

Today Was Super Plus

I've got this thing about rating days, Lord.
S is for super.
A is for average.
M is for made-it-anyway,
    and T is for terrible.
Today was S + .
It didn't start that way.
It was sort of wavering between M and T,
    first, because it was Saturday, and that means cleaning,
    and second, because I woke up feeling so down.
I knew part of the reason.
Yesterday I tried out for cheerleader,
    and didn't make it.
I was close, but not close enough.
And on top of that, this boy, Brent,
    whom I like,
    has been smiling at Pat,
    and doesn't talk to me at all.
So I was feeling really down.
Even the pancakes and papaya for breakfast didn't help,
    which was strange,
    because I love pancakes and papaya!
"What's wrong, Muffin?" Dad asked,
    pulling my hair.
"Nuthin'," I said.
Mom looked at me.
"If you could do anything you wanted to,
    what would you do today?" she asked.
"Ride a horse on the beach," I said.
I sort of surprised myself saying that.
I hadn't really thought about it too much,

but now that I had said it,
it sounded great.
Just thinking about it made me feel better.
"Why not?" Mom asked.
"I could enjoy an hour or two at the beach myself."
"Me too," Dad said grinning.
I was wondering about the cleaning,
but I thought if they'd forgotten about it,
I sure wasn't going to remind them.
But they hadn't.
"We'll all pitch in and get the cleaning done fast," Dad said.
"I'll pack a lunch," Mom said.
We had the neatest day.
We stopped to pick up Linda,
and the two of us galloped our horses up and down the beach
until both we and the horses were tired.
Then we had lunch,
and on the way home
Dad stopped and bought Mom and me some roses from one
of the boys who stands on the corner of the street and sells
them.
I gave Linda half of mine.
We had lasagna and chocolate cake for supper.
I love them both.
And then Mom and Dad played *Clue* and *Detective* with me,
and I won one game.
Afterward I told them about the cheerleading.
They waited until I had said everything I wanted to say,
and then they said
they were so sorry;
they could understand that I must have felt awful.
I didn't tell them about Brent,
because I've been thinking
maybe he'll talk to me Monday.
Dad made some cocoa with whipping cream on top
for the three of us
and then we prayed together.
Now I'm ready for bed.
I'm really amazed, Lord,
at how an M or T day
could become such a super S+ day.

Let's Think and Talk

1. What was Judy feeling about herself because she hadn't been chosen as cheerleader and because Brent wasn't paying any attention to her?
2. How did Judy's parents relate to her?
3. How did they balance responsibility with fun?
4. What made the day so special for Judy?
5. Tell about a day that you would rate S+.

A Verse to Remember

"Encourage one another, and build one another up" (1 Thess. 5:11, RSV).

14

It's Only a Ring

I didn't really mean to do it, Lord.
It was just so easy.
I was browsing through this store,
    and there were some rings for sale.
I started to try them on.
Some fit and some didn't.
I kept putting them on and taking them off.
There was this one I really liked especially much,
    so I didn't take it off.
Nobody seemed to notice.
So I wandered over to the stationery counter
    and picked up the notebook paper,
    which was why I came into the store in the first place.
There was a long line at the check-out counter,
    and the cashier
    was working fast to get everyone through.
I handed her the paper
    and the exact change.
    She bagged the paper
    and gave me the sales slip,
    and I walked out.
Just like that.
It was so easy.
But I feel funny wearing the ring,
    and somehow it doesn't look as pretty now
    as it did in the store.

Let's Think and Talk

1. What action preceded Joy's actual act of shoplifting?

48

2. Is it wrong to take something that belongs to someone else? Explain.

3. What can Joy do now?

4. Have you ever stolen anything? Do you want to tell about it?

5. What do you think God thinks about stealing?

6. Stealing a ring that is not worth much may not seem serious, but why is it?

7. What do you gain when you steal?

8. What do you lose when you steal?

9. People steal in many different ways. Talk about this.

10. What can a person do to keep from stealing?

11. Why are adults tempted to steal?

12. What is the main reason we should not steal?

A Verse to Remember

"Let him who steals steal no longer; but rather let him labor, performing with his own hands what is good, in order that he may have something to share with him who has need" (Eph. 4:28, NASB).

15

I Thought Gretchen Was Really Neat Until . . .

I sure got a surprise, Lord!
We had just moved to a different neighborhood,
    and during my first day at school
        I saw only three who had been on my softball team during
        the summer.
I wondered how I'd make friends.
Then this girl named Gretchen came up.
She's pretty
    and wears preppy clothes
    and is popular with the other kids.
"Do you play volleyball?" she asked.
I nodded.
"We need another ball player," she said.
I was glad I'm good at sports.
After that Gretchen and I were together all the time.
I thought I'd never had another friend
    so pretty
    or clever
    or wealthy
    as Gretchen.
I took her home with me one day,
    and after she left I asked Mom
    if she didn't think Gretchen was the greatest too.
Mom was busy picking up the popcorn
    Gretchen had dropped on the floor
    and gathering up her pop cans,
    so she just said, "Mmm."
Then yesterday I went home with Gretchen.
As soon as we stepped inside the kitchen,
    I heard her mom yelling,
"So that's why you're so skinny!"
She was yelling at Gretchen's brother, Philip.

"Diet pills. Why do you take diet pills?"
"I like them. They give me a high!" Philip yelled back.
"Well, you won't take them anymore!" his mother yelled.
"First your older brother on speed,
    Gretchen sneaking drinks,
    and your dad getting drunk more and more.
    What will happen to me next?"
And then I heard a loud slap,
    and someone falling and hitting something,
    and another slap
    and Philip crying.
"I've gotta be goin'," I said to Gretchen.
    "I forgot my mom told me to come straight home from school."

Let's Think and Talk

1. Why is it important to get to know both boys and girls well before we decide they are our best friends?

2. What influence do friends have on us?

3. Can your parents or counselors tell of times when they got carried away and showed poor judgment in choosing friends?

4. What do you know about LSD? Pep pills? Cocaine? Goofballs? Heroin? PCP? Alcohol? How do they affect the body? Discuss each one of these drugs and what they do to people. Do your parents know?

5. Some say they use a drug because it promises them quietness or mystical experiences. How could they experience this in a better way?

6. Some say they want to be stimulated. What better ways are there to be stimulated?

7. Some feel a need just to be different. How can people be different in constructive, rather than harmful, ways?

8. Some use drugs because they are worried about conditions in the world and want to forget about them. What is a better way to handle these anxieties?

A Verse to Remember

"Keep your heart with all vigilance;
for from it flow the springs of life" (Prov. 4:23, RSV).

16

I Was So Embarrassed!

Whew, Lord, I made it through today after all.
I'd been wondering if I would,
    what with having to give my heritage report
    in front of the whole class.
I had chosen to talk about Great-grandpa—
    where he was born,
    what he did,
    and all that.
Dad had helped me dig up a lot of information,
    and we had worked hard on putting it together.
Dad had even given me a hammer Great-grandpa had owned,
    and I had taken that to class, too.
I had my report all written out,
    but when I started to read it,
    my voice started to shake,
    and my mouth got all dry,
    and I kept wetting my lips.
I was standing behind a steel podium,
    and my knees hit it so it rattled.
I struggled through page one,
    sweating all the way,
    and turned the page,
    but my pages were mixed up.
Page two wasn't in the right place.
I started to shuffle the pages to get them in order,
    but my hands were trembling so much
    all the pages fluttered to the floor.
Everybody laughed.
I stooped to pick up the papers and knocked the hammer off the
    podium.
I could feel my face and neck getting all red.

Just then Denise, who sits in the front row, whispered,
  "Relax! It's just your English class, Tim."
I looked up and realized, of course,
  these were all my friends.
Somehow, as I had been reading the report,
  I had imagined I was in a huge room
  filled with people I didn't know.
I grinned and said,
  "Hey, just give me a second here.
  I got up a little late this morning
  and forgot to make
  sure all the papers were in order."
"Take your time," Adam said.
  His voice was kind,
  not sarcastic.
After that everything went fine,
  and my classmates said
  Great-grandpa sure was an interesting person,
  and they were glad I had told them about him.
But I never would have made it, Lord,
  if Denise and Adam hadn't reassured and encouraged me.
Thank you, Lord, for Denise and Adam.
And thank you that the rest of the day really went super good.

Let's Think and Talk

1. Why was it good that Tim had prepared as well as he had and written out his speech?

2. What one thing more could he have done to have avoided some of the confusion?

3. What could have happened if, instead of encouraging Tim, Denise had made fun of him?

4. Why do we feel small when someone laughs at us?

5. What is the difference between laughing *at* someone and laughing *with* someone? Can you give examples of this?

6. Have you ever had an embarrassing experience? Tell about it. At the time maybe you didn't think it was funny. Does it seem funny now?

7. Have your parents or teachers ever been embarrassed? Ask them to tell about it.

8. When is an embarrassment funny and when isn't it?

9. What can we learn from embarrassing experiences?

10. How do we know that Tim didn't let the embarrassing situation spoil the rest of his day?

A Verse to Remember

"Be ye kind to one another, tenderhearted" (Eph. 4:32, RSV).

17

Wendy's Abortion

I feel so bad, Lord.
Wendy's been expelled from school.
Everybody's talking about her
    and the abortion she had;
      I feel so sorry for Wendy.
I remember when the kids first started talking.
"She's getting a little bubble," they said.
"But she's only fourteen," some protested.
"She wouldn't do *that*," others said.
But she did, Lord, she did.
She lost respect from the kids
    and lost her friends.
One day she looked so sad
    I went over to talk with her.
"I didn't mean to get pregnant, honest," she said.
"I never thought that having sex a few times would do that.
    I thought sex was only for fun.
"Brett kept coaxing me.
    Finally he said, 'Well, if you don't love me . . .'
    and that did it."
"Won't your parents help you?" I asked.
"Mom's back East," she said.
    "Her divorce with Dad was finalized, and she's hurting.
    She's been with her sister two months.
I'm not sure when she'll be back.
I'm staying with a friend.
She and her mom have promised they won't tell my mom."
"But she'll find out, Wendy."
"No, she won't. I'll fix it so she won't find out."
I never guessed what she was thinking about when she said
    that, Lord.
I don't know how they found out in the school office,

but somebody must have told them
why she was absent from school for a whole week.
"We can't have this in a Christian school," the principal said,
and out Wendy went.
I wonder what will happen to her now.
And I can't figure out, Lord,
why they expelled Wendy
but let the boy stay.
They say he's even going to qualify for a sports scholarship next
year. I don't think that's fair, Lord, do you?

Let's Think and Talk

1. Wendy hadn't planned on getting pregnant. What hadn't she understood?

2. Why is there always the possibility of getting pregnant when a girl has sex with a boy?

3. Why did she finally consent to having sex with Brett?

4. When a boy asks a girl to have sex, does that mean he loves her?

5. In what way should Brett have assumed some responsibility for the pregnancy?

6. What do you think should have been done to Brett when Wendy was expelled?

7. How did Wendy's mother shirk her responsibility?

8. Instead of expelling Wendy, how could the school authorities have helped Wendy?

9. What did Wendy lose through the whole experience? What can she gain?

10. Why are abortions wrong? And dangerous?

11. What alternatives to abortion did Wendy have? What do you think Wendy should have done?

12. How could Wendy's classmates have helped her?

Verses to Remember

"A prudent man foresees the difficulties ahead and prepares for them; the simpleton goes blindly on and suffers the consequences" (Prov. 22:3, TLB).

"You shall not commit adultery" (Ex. 20:14, RSV).

18

It Isn't Always the Boy's Fault!

Why do people always think the boy is the only one at fault
    when a girl gets pregnant, Lord?
Don't they know what some of us fellows go through?
I'm so thankful you've kept me so far,
    because I've surely been tempted enough.
I wonder how many phone calls I've had?
Sometimes I've wished we could change our number
    and get an unlisted one.
And I wonder how many girls,
    wearing revealing clothes,
    have sat down on my lap
    or lain down beside me, and run their fingers through my
    hair when I'm stretched out on the grass!
It's not fair exciting a man like they do!
I'm human! Don't they know that?
It's not easy, Lord!
I don't want to be unkind,
    or act unfriendly,
    or be rude,
    but I wish the girls would cool off!
Don't they realize
    that I want to make my own choices when I'm ready
    to do so?
It's not easy, Lord.

Let's Think and Talk

1. Why do girls chase boys?

2. What kind of behavior from girls do boys find hard to deal with?

3. What excites boys sexually?

4. How would you define love?

5. One element of love is respect. How does a person show disrespect by thrusting oneself upon another?

6. Marcia calls Michael at least once every night and sometimes twice. Michael wishes she wouldn't call. He even has asked her please not to call him, but she keeps calling. What can Michael do?

7. If a girl likes a boy and wants to become better acquainted with him, what can she do that will not be offensive?

8. Why do boys back away from girls who are too bold and aggressive?

9. Ask your mother and father how they met and began to date. How did they know that they liked each other?

Verses to Remember

"Now the practices of the lower nature are clear enough: sexual immorality, impurity, sensuality. . . . I now warn you, as I have done before, that those who practice such things shall not be heirs of the kingdom of God. But the product of the Spirit is love, joy, peace, patience, kindness, goodness, faithfulness, gentleness, self-control" (Gal. 5:19-23, Williams).

19

Why Do I Have to "Mind My Manners"?

I was so surprised today, Lord,
    when I found out that Dad knows Kim's parents.
"I have them in my 'English as a Second Language class,' " he
    said.
    "They're lovely people.
    Kim's father was a dentist in their homeland.
    They had a beautiful home.
    Kim's mother studied music in France when she was young.
    They sent Kim to France for her schooling, and I think she
    was in a boarding school in England for a while, too."
I told Dad I knew.
Kim and I had started out being friends
    at the beginning of the school year.
She had told me all about their home,
    and their servants
    and their cars.
But some of the kids, who heard her talking,
    thought she was bragging,
    and they talked about how different she acted.
At the beginning of our school year
    when our teacher came into the room
    Kim would stand.
The kids used to giggle at that.
And when she would hold the door open for someone or pick up
    something someone else had dropped,
    the kids would say, "Wow! Look at Miss Manners!"
Once in a while Kim would even correct the other kids'
    grammar,
    and that really made them mad.

We all thought that she took everything too seriously—
  even P.E.
Most of us try just to relax and have fun in P.E.,
  but Kim seems to think she has to do her best
  in everything.
She thinks Americans are too laid-back.
So little by little
  the kids have been ignoring her,
  saying she thinks she's too good
  for us Americans,
  and sometimes they make fun of her.
I haven't been as friendly either as I was to begin with.
But talking with Dad has made me think.
He says he was invited to their home last night after class,
  and they started to tell him what it was like
  being transplanted to another country
  and getting used to the different ways people act.
Dad told me about some of their customs
  and mentioned how much they prize showing courtesy and
  respect.
I guess I haven't thought about this too much.
I've just expected Kim to be like another American kid.
Maybe I should try harder to understand her.
Maybe we can still be friends.
Maybe there's something I can learn from her.

Let's Think and Talk

1. What makes it difficult for people of different backgrounds to get along with each other?

2. Do you know any people who have come to North America from other countries? How well do you know them? What efforts have you made to understand them?

3. What do they find difficult about the American way of life? Why is this difficult for them?

4. Is making fun of people a kind of stealing? What do we steal from them?

5. Why do you think Kim says Americans are too laid-back? Is her observation correct? In what ways are we maybe too laid-back?

6. When people stop to visit and the TV is on, what is the courteous thing to do? Why?

7. When your parents have guests in the home, which is more courteous: (a) to converse with them; (b) to go to your room and shut your door. Explain.

8. A family had invited a number of students for dinner. One of the young men said he didn't want any dessert. He stood up, put on his headset and walked away. What was he saying to his host and hostess? How do you think they felt? How would you have handled this situation?

9. A family had been invited for dinner. The hostess served chicken and broccoli. "I don't like chicken and broccoli," one of the kids said. "Don't you have anything better?" The parents rolled their eyes. What would you have done in a situation like this if you had been (a) the boy (b) the boy's parents, (c) the hostess?

10. What difference does it make in people's opinion of us if we are courteous? Why will acting courteously and respectfully be important when we get older and look for work?

11. When we treat other people with disrespect, what are we saying to them?

Verses to Remember

"When a stranger resides with you in your land, you shall not do him wrong. The stranger who resides with you shall be to you as the native among you, and you shall love him as yourself. . . . I am the Lord your God" (Lev. 19:33, 34, NASB).

20

My Mother Is an Alcoholic

Mom is an alcoholic, Lord.
I haven't even dared put it in words before,
   but I honestly believe she is.
If she isn't an alcoholic,
   when I come home from school
   why do I find her lying on the sofa,
   still dressed in her bathrobe,
   her hair a mess,
   and she half asleep?
If she isn't an alcoholic,
   why do I find empty liquor bottles in the trash can,
   and unopened bottles hidden all over the house?
I don't think anybody else knows, Lord.
I know the people at church don't.
Mom is president of the women's club,
   and she goes to Bible class.
Nobody would dream she's an alcoholic—
   she would never take a drink in front of her church friends.
Dad's work keeps him away from home a lot,
   and when Mom knows he's coming home,
   she's never drunk.
I love Mom so much, Lord,
   even if it makes me feel both sick and ashamed
   every time I find her drunk.
What can I do to help her, Lord?

Let's Think and Talk

1. How can we know a person is an alcoholic?
2. What can be done to help an alcoholic admit he or she is one?

3. What can be done to help motivate an alcoholic to get help?

4. What benefits come from drinking?

5. What heartaches come when drinking gets out of control?

6. How does alcoholism develop?

7. Is the statement "I can control my drinking" true for everyone?

8. What help is there for families of an alcoholic?

9. What is the surest way for a person not to become an alcoholic?

Verses to Remember

"Call upon me in the day of trouble; I will deliver you, and you shall glorify me" (Ps. 51:15, RSV).

"Don't let the sparkle and the smooth taste of strong wine deceive you. For in the end it bites like a poisonous serpent; it stings like an adder" (Prov. 23:31, 32, TLB).

21

So What, If I Didn't Get My Work Done?

Today started out being so good
    and ended up being so bad, Lord.
Lisa called early this morning.
She wanted me to go with her to the beach.
"May I, Mom?" I asked,
    holding my hand over the mouthpiece of the phone.
    "Please. I want to."
"Sure," Mom said,
    "after you've washed the dishes,
    straightened up the house,
    and taken out the trash.
    You can help me with dinner when I get home from work.
    Dad'll be home around 10 this morning.
    Maybe he'll take you."
Super! I thought.
I biked to the store to pick up some pop and chips
    and watched TV when I came home.
As soon as I heard Dad's car in the driveway,
    I flew out,
    beach bag and cooler in hand.
I dumped them down
    and flung myself into Dad's arms,
    laughing and hugging him.
"Please, Dad, take me to the beach, will you?
    Mom said I could go.
    Lisa's goin' too.
    We can pick her up, can't we?"
Dad grinned.
    "Okay, Muffin," he said,
    rumpling my hair.

I was hot and sandy
    when I dragged myself into the house
    around 5:30.
My sunburn was hurtin' bad.
The kitchen counter
    and the sink,
    cluttered with dirty, dried-out dishes
    and a fly buzzing around them,
    greeted me.
The sugar and milk were still on the table,
    the bread in the basket
    was curling at the edges.
In the family room I saw the newpapers scattered
    and empty pop cans
    and popcorn from last night
    on the floor.

"What a dump to come home to!" I grumbled.
"That's what I thought, too." Mom had walked into the kitchen.
Her voice was sort of unsteady.
"Lori, didn't I ask you . . ."
    she began.
I knew what was coming,
    so I just shuffled down the hall,
    dragging my towel.
Lord, why do I have to do everything?
    Why can't Tom clean up the house?
    Or Dad take out the trash?
    Or Mom do it herself?
And why do I feel so down tonight?
The day started out so well.
What a rotten way for it to end!

Let's Think and Talk

1. What attitude did Lori's mother sense when Lori came home?

2. If you had been Lori's mother, what would you have done?

3. How would you answer Lori's question as to why others couldn't do the dishes, pick up, take out the trash, etc.?

4. Why do you think Lori was feeling so down?

5. What could she have done so she could have gone to bed happy?

6. When your parents ask you to do something and you don't, what are some of the reasons?

7. How will your reactions toward your parents *now* affect your life in the *future*?

8. Often we hurt others and ourselves simply because we are thoughtless. We don't take time to think. Discuss how this has happened in your family sometimes.

A Verse to Remember

"He who is faithful in a very little thing is faithful also in much; and he who is unrighteous in a very little thing is unrighteous also in much" (Luke 16:10, NASB).

22

Rod Gives Me the Creeps

Dear God, how can I deal with someone
    who's always mean?
There's a guy at school, Rod,
    who, just because he's trained to be a junior policeman,
    thinks he's so great!
He's always talking so big,
    threatening kids with, "I'm gonna turn you in for this."
Or if someone tries to get even with him,
    he taunts,
    "Go ahead, hit me,
    and I'll turn you in!"
Last week Dale had some grass in his pocket that sorta looked
    like dope "grass" but wasn't.
Rod knew it wasn't "grass,"
    but he reported it to the principal.
The principal called the police and Dale's mother.
They came storming right into our math class.
Dale's mother was all red-eyed.
The police took Dale away and
Rod sat grinning.
After class when we were outside,
    he started to laugh.
"Hey! Did you see what I did?" he sneered.
I was mad—so, so mad, Lord!
"How could you do that?" I asked.
I was shaking all over.
"What a mean, mean thing to do!"
"Yeah!" the other kids said.
    "Get out of here, Rod!
    We don't need you."
After that, every time Rod came around,
    everybody yelled,

"Go away! We don't want you."
The next day Rod threw a book out the window.
And at noon he got on Julie's case.
    She was wearing a new outfit,
    a really pretty one.
"You sure look ugly today," Rod said.
"Whatcha done to your hair?" he asked me.
    "Put it in a vacuum cleaner?"
It's hard to like him when he says things like that, Lord.
But I kinda worry about him too.
What'll happen to him if he doesn't change?

Let's Think and Talk

1. Why do you think Rod talked like he did?

2. Have you met anyone like him?

3. Why do you think he threw a book out the window?

4. Some kids are angry and mean habitually. What does that possibly show is missing in their lives?

5. What can be done to help them?

6. When is confronting people about wrong behavior helpful?

7. What can we always do if we're concerned about people but don't know how to help them?

8. Do you remember a time when you lost your temper? Why did you lose it? Did you have to lose it?

9. If losing our temper is wrong, what can we do to control it when we are angry?

10. Is it possible to lose our temper without hurting someone? Explain.

Verses to Remember

"But I say to you who hear, love your enemies, do good to those who hate you" (Luke 6:27, NASB).

"Be angry, and yet do not sin; do not let the sun go down on your anger, and do not give the devil an opportunity" (Eph. 4:26, 27, NASB).

23

_I'm_ in the Minority!

I can't get used to how different this school is, Lord.
When I went to elementary school,
    at Christmastime everyone talked
    about Santa Claus,
    and gifts and Christmas trees.
At my junior high last year,
    we focused more on the real meaning of Christmas.
We did a drama about Christ's birth and sang carols.
But here in my new school, Lord,
    nobody talks about anything religious.
Instead, the kids talk about our two weeks' winter vacation.
Of course I realize one reason is
    so many of the kids have different religions
    and some don't have any at all.
But it sure feels strange.
It makes me feel . . . empty . . . and sad,
    and I'm beginning to realize
    that not everyone is a Christian,
    and Christmas doesn't mean something
    personal to everybody.
I know there aren't too many "all-out-for-Jesus Christians,"
    but so many of the kids in school
    don't believe in Jesus or God at all.
Even those whom you would think are Christians
    don't go to church
    or do any of the things
    I'd expect Christians would do.
It makes me feel like a real minority.
I wonder how you feel, Lord.

Let's Think and Talk

1. How many nationality groups are represented in your school?

2. What religions do your classmates follow?

3. Have you ever asked one of them to tell you about his religion, what he believes about God?

4. How can we show others respect even if we don't believe what they believe?

5. When someone asks you what Christians believe, what do you answer?

6. One girl said: "I felt that Rachel was interested in being my friend only as long as she thought she could convert me to Christianity. When she realized I wasn't going to change my religion, she stopped being my friend." Discuss this observation.

A Verse to Remember

"I will also make you a light of the nations, so that my salvation may reach to the end of the earth" (Isa. 49:6).

Discuss how we can be "lights."

24

Sometimes I Need Help

Dear God,
My mom's the greatest!
I wanted to join the church as an adult member,
    and our pastor asked
    if I'd give a testimony at the Sunday morning service.
I love you so much, Jesus,
    and I wanted to tell others
    what you've done for me,
    but still I was scared.
All those people!
"I'll help you prepare," Mom said.
She planned it so that on Mother's Day weekend
    just the two of us
    went up to the mountains
    for a Mother's Day retreat.
It was so great having a whole weekend
    with Mom all to myself.
I couldn't believe it!
We worked on my talk together,
    and Mom was a big help.
On Sunday when I gave it,
    I felt all shaky,
    but it went fine.
People thanked me afterward.
One lady said,
    "God loves us very much, doesn't He?"
All I could do was nod my head
    'cuz I was all choked up.
Mom hugged me tightly and said,
    "I'm so proud of you! You did very well."
I was so happy, Lord!
I felt so close to people.

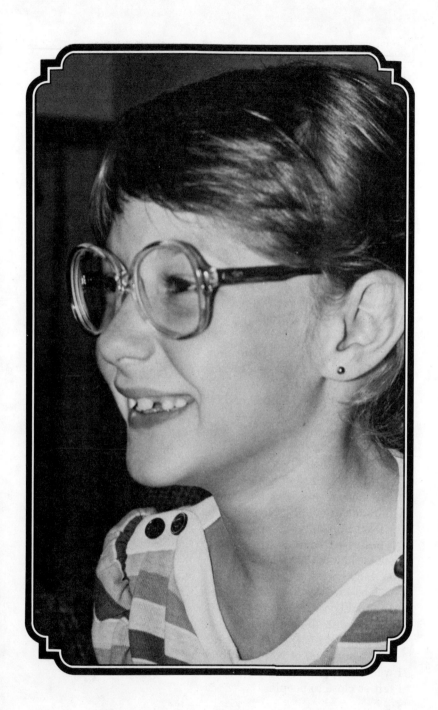

Our family went out for lunch after church.
I was so happy I felt like dancing.
I love you so much, Jesus!
With you and my parents helping me,
    nothing can go wrong.
At least that's the way I feel now.
Thank you, Lord, thank you!

Let's Think and Talk

1. How did Jody show she was a responsible person?
2. How did Jody's mother show that she respected Jody?
3. What made Jody feel close to the people at church?
4. What made her feel close to Jesus?
5. Have you had any similar experiences?
6. Have your parents had similar experiences? Talk about this together.

Verses to Remember

"Let no one despise your youth, but set the believers an example in speech and conduct, in love, in faith, in purity" (1 Tim. 4:12, RSV).

"Now concerning spiritual gifts, brethren, I do not want you to be uninformed. . . . And God has appointed in the church . . . helpers" (1 Cor. 12:1, 28, RSV).

25

Sometimes I Feel Left Out

The kids played volleyball again today
  when the youth group got together at church.
Volleyball leaves me out.
How can I play when I can't see?
Most of the time I don't mind.
I sit with the adults and talk.
But today, after a while, the adults wandered off to the kitchen
    to get the food ready,
      and I was left alone.
I sat and listened to the sound of the ball
    being batted back and forth,
    and the shuffling of feet on the pavement,
    and the voices calling to each other,
      and I felt all alone.
I began to feel pretty worthless too.
I couldn't play,
    and I'd only be in the way in the kitchen.
One of the adults came back to see how the game was going,
    and I asked him if he'd guide me to the fellowship hall and
    the piano.
I sat down and began to play.
I played and played,
    and got so lost in the music
    I didn't hear some of the kids come in.
When the last notes died,
    I felt them there, near me: Peter, Meghan, Steve and Carrie.
"That was great, Jeanne!" Pete said. "Play some more!"
I did.
They began to sing.
Then one of the counselors put her hands on my shoulders and
    said,

"Let's ask Jeanne if she'll play for our Parents' Banquet, shall we?"

"Hey, yeah! That would be great!" they all said.

"And now, let's eat," the counselor said.

"Lead me to it," I said.

That's one thing I can do with the kids.

Let's Think and Talk

1. Why did Jeanne feel left out?
2. How did she try to control her feelings?
3. Why did playing the piano help her feel better?
4. How did the other youth show their affection for Jeanne?
5. How did the counselor show her respect for Jeanne?
6. Do you ever feel left out? When and why?
7. How do you control your feelings?
8. What do you do to help yourself retain a sense of self-worth?
9. What special gift has God given you? How are you developing it?
10. Is there anyone in your youth group whom you think feels left out? What can you do about it? Talk about this.

Verses to Remember

Read Matthew 25:14–29 and discuss this parable.

"Give, and it will be given to you; good measure, pressed down, shaken together, running over, they will pour into your lap. For whatever measure you deal out to others, it will be dealt to you in return" (Luke 6:38, NASB).

26

Whispering Wind's Choice

Today was Dad's day off.
He went to the Indian reservation to repair some of the washing
    machines that had broken down.
"Want to go with me, Susie?" he asked.
My dad's the only one who can call me Susie.
I make sure everybody else calls me Suzanne.
"And miss school?" I asked.
"Once won't hurt," he said. "I'll talk to your teacher."
When we came to the reservation
    we found Whispering Wind,
        the famous Indian singer there.
What a surprise!
She was all dressed up in Indian costume,
    and she sang for about an hour
    and told Indian folk tales
    and explained what life was like many years ago
    and how proud they could be they were Indians.
The kids listened so intently that one little fellow,
    who kept moving to the edge of his chair,
        actually fell off!
He didn't cry though.
Instead, he picked himself up
    and stood straight and tall and said,
        "Whispering Wind, when I grow up, I'm going to be great
    like you!"
And Whispering Wind reached down and hugged him,
    and her face just shone.
"I'm sure you will be great," she said.
    "You're already special.
    You're Indian, and even more important,
    you're made by God."

On the way home Dad and I were talking about how
    Whispering Wind, who is so famous,
      wouldn't have to think about the Indians on the reservation
    or come to them once a month like she does.
We talked about how much it meant to the Indians that
    she did come,
    and how Whispering Wind's face glowed.
I wonder, Lord,
    what could I do to encourage someone as Whispering Wind
    does?

Let's Think and Talk

1. Judging by the way he spent his day off, what do we know about Suzanne's dad's values?

2. How did Suzanne's dad show his affection for her?

3. Why did it mean so much to the Indians on the reservation to have Whispering Wind come to them?

4. What did Whispering Wind value more than fame and comfort?

5. What answer do you think the Lord would give you if you prayed Suzanne's prayer?

Verses to Remember

"Do nothing from selfishness or empty conceit, but with humility of mind let each of you regard one another as more important than himself; do not merely look out for your own personal interests, but also for the interests of others. Have this attitude in yourselves, which was also in Christ Jesus, who, although He existed in the form of God, did not regard equality with God a thing to be grasped, but emptied Himself, taking the form of a bondservant" (Phil. 2:3–7, NASB).

Discuss the meaning of these verses.

27

Oh, Come On! Light Up!

Dear Lord,
>   One thing's sure:
>   I don't ever want to smoke!
I think it's so dumb to harm your body.
Today in school a doctor showed us
>   how the heart speeds up
>   and has to work harder
>   as soon as you light up a cigarette.
Smokers say a cigarette calms them,
>   but on the screen it showed
>   how jumpy the nervous system becomes.
The doctor showed pictures of smokers' lungs.
>   The lungs had become so diseased and black they had to be
>   removed.
>   He also showed pictures of a man who had undergone
>   surgery because of throat cancer.
Yuk! It was awful!
It made me mad to think of all those tobacco companies
>   making money and getting rich
>   while ruining people's health.
I never want to work for a tobacco company!
Mom says she wishes she had never started smoking.
She's having an awful time stopping.
She succeeds only for a little while.
She's gone to treatment centers
>   and taken pills
>   and done the whole bit.
How awful, Lord, to be a slave like that.
Dad used to smoke,
>   but his heart attack was so scary
>   he quit "cold turkey."

He says he doesn't want to die this young.
Strange how Dad could quit, but Mom can't.
But Phil and I've agreed we're never, never going to light up.
"Please don't," Mom says.
   "I don't want you to go through what I am."
Dear God, will you help Mom find the help she needs?
Then she won't cough and have to worry about cancer,
   and our house will smell sweet and fresh and clean,
   not stale like it does now.

Let's Think and Talk

1. What do tobacco companies value most?

2. What do tobacco companies do in their advertisements to persuade people to smoke? Study some ads in magazines.

3. What do people who smoke value most?

4. Do you know anyone who has had a heart attack or lung cancer because of smoking? If possible, talk with him.

5. What does cigarette smoking do for a person?

6. What does not smoking do for a person?

7. When a person has been a habitual smoker and then tries to stop, how does he or she feel physically? Ask someone who is trying to stop.

8. In what way can receiving correct information help us to make wise decisions?

Verses to Remember

"Do you not know that you are a temple of God, and that the Spirit of God dwells in you?" (1 Cor. 3:16, NASB).

"I urge you therefore, brethren, by the mercies of God, to present your bodies a living and holy sacrifice, acceptable to God, which is your spiritual service of worship" (Rom. 12:1, NASB).

28

My Special Friend

Lord, you've done the neatest thing for me!
Ever since my face started to break out in acne,
    I've hated the way I look.
"What's wrong with you? Have you got chicken pox?"
    one of the guys at Sunday school asked.
I felt like I had leprosy.
When I looked at myself in the mirror,
    I wondered how any girl would ever like a guy with a face
    like mine.
And that's the fantastic thing that has happened, Lord.
Jill, the smartest girl in our class;
    Jill, with the warm, brown eyes and smooth, shining hair;
    Jill, the tennis whiz;
    Jill . . . likes *me*!
"When Suk came to our school and couldn't speak much English
    and dressed so poorly
    and was so different in every way,
    you were a friend to him," she said to me.
"Shucks," I said, "that was nothing.
    Suk needed a friend."
"When Jeanne was sick for so long,
    you brought her homework to her every night
    and even helped her when she had trouble with some of her
    assignments."
"Shucks," I said, "that was nothing.
    "Poor Jeanne. It was tough being sick so long."
"When you chose not to play basketball
    (she didn't say anything about why I didn't,
    but with all the acne on my back, how could I play?),
    you still went to every game and cheered the loudest."
"Shucks," I said, "that was nothing.

I wanted the team to win."
"Every morning when I see you,
   you have a big smile on your face," she said.
"Why not?" I asked, grinning. "Jesus loves me, and I love Him."
"I do, too," she said,
   "So that makes two of us.
   So why shouldn't we be friends?"
It's too good to be true, Lord.
I can't believe it. Me. With my acne.

Let's Think and Talk

1. Why did John think none of the girls would like him?
2. How did Jill show her maturity in choosing a friend?
3. What did Jill see in John that she appreciated?
4. What did Jill's friendship mean to John?
5. What qualities do you look for in a friend?
6. How important is physical appearance? Clothes? Money?
7. Why do so many place high priority on physical appearance?
8. What influences them?
9. Ask your mother and father or your counselors what they valued most about each other when they became friends.

A Verse to Remember

"But the Lord said to Samuel, 'Do not look at his appearance or at the height of his stature, because I have rejected him; for God sees not as man sees, for man looks at the outward appearance, but the Lord looks at the heart' " (1 Sam. 16:7, NASB).

29

Your Mother <u>Cleans Houses</u>?

Dad's been out of work for more than a year,
    and there are no more unemployment checks.
We all knew Mom would have to find a job,
    but did it have to be cleaning houses, Lord?
I was so embarrassed I almost died.
When the kids at school asked
    if she had found a job,
    I said,
    "Yes, interior decorating.
    She goes from house to house."
I knew that wasn't what it really was,
    and I sure hoped the word wouldn't get back to Mom,
    or that someone would call and ask for her interior
    decorating services.
Because Mom goes to work every day,
    Dad and I have had to clean *our* house.
Funny thing, but I'm discovering
    I almost enjoy it, Lord!
It's fun working with Dad.
And I like to see the furniture shining
    and the windows sparkling.
Randy, my kid brother, complains that
    I'm getting as fussy as Mom,
    yelling at him to keep his room in order.
But I *like* the feeling I get when everything is in order.
Next, I think I'll try cooking.

Let's Think and Talk

1. Why did Mike find it embarrassing to tell his friends that

his mother was cleaning houses?

2. Why do some people consider, for example, doing secretarial work more acceptable than doing housework? What is the difference?

3. What jobs are considered desirable? Why? Which ones are considered undesirable? Why?

4. What could help to bring a greater sense of dignity and value to doing housework?

5. What examples do we see here of a family pulling together?

6. Is it important to you what kind of work your parents and your friends' parents do? Discuss this.

A Verse to Remember

"Whatever you do in word or deed, do all in the name of the Lord Jesus, giving thanks through Him to God the Father" (Col. 3:17, NASB).

30

Who Wants to Dig Weeds?

I'm feeling grumpy, Lord.
Today's Saturday.
Randy and I had planned on getting up early and going fishing,
    but Mom said, "No fishing until you get the garden
    in back dug up so I can plant."
Does she know how long that will take?
Of course, I guess she has been on my case to do it
    the last three weeks,
        ever since the weather suddenly turned so nice,
        and I guess if I had worked at it little by little
        it would have been done long ago;
        but there have been so many other fun things to do with the
        kids.
Besides, I *hate* digging.
"When you get a job, chances are there'll always be some things
    you'll hate doing," Mom said quietly.
    "So you might as well start now to learn to do something
    you don't particularly enjoy if that is your responsibility."
I wish she'd quit preaching!
So what do I do now, Lord?
I can't go fishing until it's done,
    so . . . I guess I've no choice.
Wonder how long it will take me?
Wonder if I can get done today if I work hard?
There's a ball game tonight.
Do you suppose Dad would go with me, Lord?
That would be neat!
If I could go to the ball game tonight,
    I wouldn't mind working today.
I could even pay for our tickets with what I earn.
Thanks for the idea, Lord.
I'd better go look for Dad.

Let's Think and Talk

1. Why had Ken procrastinated in digging up the vegetable garden?

2. Why did his mother say he should do it?

3. What solution did he arrive at that helped make it easier to do the unpleasant?

4. How did being able to buy the tickets make him feel?

5. Have you ever experienced a conflict between wanting to do something fun and doing your duty? Tell about it.

6. What was the result?

7. Why does acting responsibly, and in this case, acting in obedience to a parent, give us a feeling of well-being?

8. With whom are we in harmony when we obey?

9. Have you ever noticed the relationship between obedience, self-respect and feeling good, or disobedience and feeling unhappy? Talk about this.

10. If it is true that we feel better when we walk according to God's guidelines, why do we rebel?

11. What character traits do we show we lack by not acting responsibly or doing our duty?

A Verse to Remember

"He who is faithful in a very little thing is faithful also in much; and he who is unrighteous in a very little thing is unrighteous also in much" (Luke 16:10, NASB).

31

Mom Had Surgery

Mom had surgery yesterday.
What an experience, Lord!
Waiting for the doctor
    to come with the report
    was terrible.
"What time is it?" I'd ask Dad.
He'd tell me.
"What time is it?" I'd ask again,
    after only five minutes had passed.
I never knew time could pass so slowly.
And I've never felt so relieved as I did
    when the doctor finally came
    and said everything was all right.
Whoosh!
I let out the longest breath,
    and then I had to go to the bathroom.
But I tightened up all over again
    when I saw Mom as they wheeled her into her room
    afterward.
She sure didn't look all right to me.
"She'll look better tomorrow, son," Dad said,
    and he was right.
I couldn't believe the change!
Today she was sitting up in bed,
    smiling and eating,
    and her hair was combed,
    and her cheeks were pink,
    and she looked real pretty.
What a change!
I really meant it when I breathed a prayer of thanks to you,
    Lord.

My Indian friend, Prem Bahadur, went with me
    to the hospital today.
Dad was at work, and I didn't want to go alone.
As we were waiting for the bus to go home,
    Prem said wishfully,
    "North America is such a wonderful place!
    Your hospitals are so clean and well-equipped, and you have
    so many of them.
    Your doctors and nurses are well-trained.
    You never run out of medicine."
I felt awkward.
"Is it different in India?" I asked.
Prem smiled a sad little smile.
"So different," he said.
    "You wouldn't understand if I told you.
    But maybe someday you can visit me, and then you'll know."

Let's Think and Talk

1. Why was visiting his mother in the hospital a good experience for Jeff? What understanding did he gain?

2. How could this understanding help him in the future?

3. How does it help to know what's going on in a "worrying" situation?

4. What did the experience do for Jeff's relationship to his mother?

5. How did Prem Bahadur's remarks give Jeff new understanding of how wealthy he was? Spend a little time trying to imagine what it would be like to be sick and live in a country where there were no hospitals or doctors close enough for you to reach. Or suppose you heard of a hospital 100 miles away and had to be carried there on someone's back, over mountain paths. Talk about what arrangements would have to be made, and what the experience would be like.

6. Has anyone in your family been in the hospital or had surgery? Discuss what the experience meant to each of you.

Verses to Remember

"Be anxious for nothing, but in everything by prayer and

supplication with thanksgiving let your requests be made known to God. And the peace of God, which surpasses all comprehension, shall guard your hearts and your minds in Christ Jesus" (Phil. 4:6, 7, NASB).

32

Discovering Our Roots

We just came back from the neatest vacation, Lord.
To begin with, when Mom and Dad were talking about it,
    I thought it would be so boring.
I didn't want to go.
But it wasn't boring at all.
We drove all the way back to New Jersey
    where my grandparents and great-grandparents once lived.
Aunt Mabel still lives there in a 150-year-old house.
One day we went creaking up the stairs to her attic.
There she opened a hump-backed trunk
    and took out from it
    all sorts of pictures in stiff, brown, cardboard frames
    and told us all about our family from 'way back when.
She had Great-grandma's wedding dress all wrapped up in
    tissue paper.
Great-granny was Amish,
    and her wedding dress was gray-blue.
There was a ruffled bonnet in the trunk, too.
Do you suppose Great-granny wore a bonnet for her wedding?
Aunt Mabel's a fascinating storyteller,
    and she made all our ancestors seem so real
    that we could just picture them.
Life sure was tough for them.
They had to work so hard and had so little.
We began to understand why Grandma saves everything:
    string,
    wrapping paper,
    rubber bands—
    everything.
She does a lot better than we do at saving newspaper,
    glass and aluminum cans for recycling,

and she still has a compost pit in her backyard for her
  garbage.
I understand now why she does all this.
She had so little when she grew up,
  and it was hard getting what she had.
I've been thinking, Lord,
  maybe I should start a chest
  and get pictures of all our family from 'way back when
  and write down what Aunt Mabel told me.
When Grandma comes for her next visit,
  I know what we'll talk about.
I'll ask her to tell me how it was when she was a little girl,
  and how she met Grandpa,
  and where her kids were born—
  was she in a hospital or at home—
  and what troubles did Grandpa and she have.
The more I think about it,
  the more excited I get about learning more about my family.
Thank you, Lord, for families.

Let's Think and Talk

1. How did gaining information help Denise in her relationship to her grandparents?

2. Learning about her family also gave Denise a feeling of
belonging. What do you know about your extended family?

3. What prompted Denise to want to begin a history chest?

4. Where were your grandparents born? What did they do?
How many children did they have?

5. Where were your parents born? How did they meet?
Maybe you will want to encourage them to tell you about their
childhood.

A Verse to Remember

"But the lovingkindness of the Lord is from everlasting to
everlasting on those who fear him, and His righteousness to
children's children" (Ps. 103:17, NASB).

(The margin gives the alternate word "revere" for "fear."
Discuss the meaning of this verse.)

33

My Bike Was Stolen

I came out from school yesterday,
    and my bike was gone!
I couldn't believe it.
I had locked it as always.
When I told Dad, his brow puckered,
    and he said,
    "Let's go down to school."
He stood looking around, then said,
    "Mary, I wonder if it could have been someone from the high
    school down the block.
    Someone from your school
    would be afraid to ride it to school because
    you could identify it and the person could be caught.
    Tell you what we'll do.
    I'll leave work for an hour tomorrow and meet you here, just
    before the school gets out.
    We should have someone from the high school with us—
    someone who knows the kids."
"How about Richard?" I asked.
    Richard's our neighbor
    and he's a ninth grader."
"Good idea!" Dad said.
Richard said, "Sure, I'll help you,"
    when I explained to him what had happened.
So today Dad and I went over to the high school
    before the classes were dismissed.
"Let's see if we can find your bike," Dad said.
We walked up and down the rows of bikes,
    and sure enough, there was mine
    right in the middle.
I got so excited.

"Look, Dad," I said, "same old bump on the back fender,
   and the orange sticker is still on the seat."
"And the license plate is still on," Dad said.
"Okay," Dad continued,
   "now we'll go over by the gate and wait and watch."
A couple minutes later a bell rang, and the kids came
   streaming out.
Richard walked over and joined us.
We watched carefully.
Then we saw a boy
   headed right for my bike.
Just as he stooped down to unlock it,
   he looked up and saw us.
He dropped the lock and walked away,
   trying to act real casual.
"Recognize him, Richard?" Dad asked.
"Sure," Richard said and gave the boy's name.
We waited.
One by one the kids wheeled through the gate,
   and my bike was left alone, unclaimed.
"Now you go and stand by it,
   and I'll go to the principal's office," Dad said.
He had the receipt for the license,
   and when the principal checked the lock,
   he found it was one that had been reported stolen.
The principal said he would take care of things from here on.
He unlocked my bike,
   and I rode it home.
Was I ever glad to get it back again!
But I wonder what will happen to the boy.

Let's Think and Talk

   1. What do you think will happen to the boy?
   2. Why do you think he stole?
   3. Have you ever been tempted to steal?
   4. What tempted you?
   5. Some people help themselves to stationery and office sup-
plies or tools or whatever they use at work. Is this stealing?
What is their reasoning?

6. Read Exodus 20:15, 17. What does "covet" mean?

7. Read Jeremiah 22:13–17 in The Living Bible Version if you have it. Read also James 5:1–5. Why do some people steal? How does a family suffer when one member of the family steals?

8. When we do something wrong, our conscience pricks us. We feel uncomfortable and unhappy. Why is it more important to keep a good conscience than to possess a lot of things?

9. What does the Bible teach us happened to Jesus because of our sin? (Isa. 53:5). Do you think God still suffers when we sin?

Verses to Remember

"You shall not steal" (Ex. 20:15, NASB).

"A life of doing right is the wisest life there is. If you live that kind of life, you'll not limp or stumble as you run" (Prov. 4:11, 12, TLB).

"Some rich people are poor, and some poor people have great wealth!" (Prov. 13:7, TLB).

Discuss the meaning of this verse.

34

Todd's Weird

Dear God,
I feel sorry for Todd.
He's really smart,
    and in some ways he's nice.
He isn't pushy when we stand in line at the cafeteria,
    and he doesn't use bad language.
But in other ways he acts so different
    that the kids think he's weird.
He's got this thing about collecting aluminum cans,
    and every chance he gets
    he goes through all the trash cans
    digging out aluminum cans.
If he likes a girl,
    he doesn't know how to show it,
    but instead he comes up behind her,
    puts his thumbs in his ears, waves his hands and growls to
    scare her.
I feel sorry for him, Lord,
    but I don't know what to do.

Let's Think and Talk

1. How could Todd's classmates help him?
2. What is meant by "socially acceptable"?
3. How can acting in a way that is socially acceptable strengthen our other gifts and abilities?
4. How can acting in a way that is socially acceptable help when we are witnessing of our faith in Jesus?
5. What is the difference between being "socially acceptable" and doing everything our peers want us to do so we will be accepted?

A Verse to Remember

"Only conduct yourselves in a manner worthy of the gospel of Christ" (Phil. 1:27, NASB).

35

I Got a Job!

Well, I finally found a job, Lord.
Thank you.
You know how I've been praying about this
    ever since three weeks ago
    when Dad said,
    "You're old enough to find some kind of job away from home."
At first I was so shocked
    I couldn't believe Dad really meant it.
But he did.
Then I wondered what I could do,
    and how I'd ever find work
    when work is so hard to find,
    and I'm not even sixteen yet.
Then I remembered how Sis had worked in a doughnut shop,
    so I stopped to see Mrs. Young.
"You are too young to wait on customers," she said,
    "but we need someone to mop the floors
    and scrub the counters and tables,
    wash the racks and the glass in the display case
    and clean up the back room.
Do you think you could do that?"
"Why not?" I asked.
"I'll give you a week to show me," she said.
I hadn't realized how tired my arms would get
    or what it would be like to have to go to work every evening,
    or how long it would take me,
    but I'm learning.
Mrs. Young told me tonight the job is mine.
I had thought I could spend the money I earned
    anyway I wanted,
    and I was getting pretty excited about this.

I got another shock from Dad last night.

"You might as well learn wise money management right from the beginning," he told me.

"I hope you'll want to give a tithe to the Lord like Mom and I have done all these years.

A certain percentage each week should be put in savings.

I suggest you also start to buy some of your clothes."

Dad gave me a book, too, and said I should record both my income and expenditures,

the money I give away and spend.

I'm still getting used to this whole idea, Lord.

It's like a new adventure.

Let's Think and Talk

1. What are the benefits for a kid who works?

2. How old do you think kids should be when they start to work?

3. Is it reasonable to expect kids to put some money in savings? To buy some of their clothes?

4. If kids want brand-name clothes, and parents feel they can't afford to buy brand names, what can be done?

5. How much financial help do your parents plan to give you toward higher education? Toward purchasing a car? Toward operating a car and paying insurance?

6. What is a tithe? If your parents tithe, ask them to tell you what it has meant to them to do so.

7. Ask your parents how old they were when they started to work. What work did they do? How much did they earn? What did they spend their money for?

8. What benefit is it for kids if parents do not pay all their higher education expenses?

Verses to Remember

"Honor the Lord by giving him the first part of all your income, and he will fill your barns with wheat and barley and overflow your wine vats with the finest wines" (Prov. 3:9, 10, TLB).

36

I Don't Want Another Father!

I hate Harold!
I'll never call him Dad.
Why do I need another father?
I already have one,
    and I like the one I have.
I wasn't the one who decided Dad wouldn't live with us
    anymore.
If I had my way,
    he'd still be home.
And now, as though it wasn't bad enough

not to have Dad home,
Mom's married Harold;
and he's moved in with us,
and I'm supposed to call him Dad!
Never!
I don't even want to talk to him.
He's got it in for me, I can tell.
Mom used to let me stay up till midnight.
Harold says school kids should be in bed by 10:00,
and he's got Mom on his side,
so now they're both against me.
Mom used to give me money
so I could pick up whatever food I wanted
and eat whenever I wanted to.
But now, all of a sudden, Mom is saying that
doughnuts
and French fries
and Cokes
and potato chips
and Twinkies,
and all the things I like, aren't good for me.
How come she changed all of a sudden?
I'll bet that's Harold's doing too.
Mom says I should be happy
we have a complete family again,
but I don't see it that way.
I hate Harold!

Let's Think and Talk

1. Why do you think Joel's mother welcomed remarriage? What difference did it make for her?

2. How did Joel view Harold?

3. Why did Joel not welcome the marriage?

4. Many people give extra loving care and attention to children caught in the stressful situation of parents' divorce. This is important. However, when this leads to pampering, this "affection" can hurt. What do you think the difference is between pampering and loving a child?

5. A new parent may not give in to a child's demands as easily as the child is used to. What does this feel like to the child? Why?

6. The Bible tells us that one of the principles of life is "whatever a man sows, this he will also reap." How is this principle true in relationships?

7. What will help Joel in his situation?

Verses to Remember

"Whoever loves discipline loves knowledge,
but he who hates reproof is stupid" (Prov. 12:1, NASB).

"The way of a fool is right in his own eyes,
but a wise man is he who listens to counsel" (Prov. 11:15, NASB).

37

I Hate Harold!

I hate Harold.
I hate the way he tries to be so nicey-nice to me
    while at the same time
    he's making life miserable for me
    with all his rules:
    in bed on school nights at ten,
    only parental-permitted TV shows,
    and none until the homework is done,
    no allowance if chores aren't done,
    on time for meals.
Yuk! What a life!
I finally decided I'd show him a thing or two.
Last night I sneaked into his closet and cut the bottom out of
    the pockets of his dress slacks.
This morning, when he put his billfold and keys in his pockets,
    they all fell through.
He put on another pair of pants
    and the same thing happened.
Boy, was he mad!
Mom grabbed a pair
    and quickly sewed up the pockets on the machine,
    and said they'd talk to me
    when they came home tonight.
Then Harold went to back his car out of the garage.
I had gone out there last night
    and turned on the lights
    so the battery would run down.
You should have heard Harold!
If he's supposed to be such a great Christian,
    why does he get so mad?
"Joel," he said,

spacing each word
and dipping it in ice,
"for some reason you've decided not to like me.
Maybe you can't help the way you feel toward me.
Maybe you can, but won't.
But just because you feel mean toward me
  does not justify the mean things you're doing."
Now what did he mean by that?
If I can't express what I feel,
  what am I supposed to do?

Let's Think and Talk

1. How would you answer Joel's question?

2. Why do you think Joel feels the way he does toward Harold?

3. If you were Harold, what would you do about the situation?

4. Do you know anyone who is a stepchild? Would he be willing to tell what it was like to get a stepparent?

Verses to Remember

"Hatred stirs up strife, but love covers all transgressions" (Prov. 10:12, NASB).

"Doing wickedness is like sport to a fool" (Prov. 10:23, NASB).

38

I Wish Our House Was Nicer

My sister Carol was so embarrassed
    she said she thought she'd die.
There's a boy, Mike,
    that she likes a lot.
Mike's dad is an executive of some big corporation,
    and they live in a mansion in Secluded Gardens.
Everyone says their house is just gorgeous.
Anyway, when Mike asked Carol for a date
    she said to me,
    "I can't have him come *here* to pick me up.
    Not to our little house in *this* neighborhood."
So she arranged with her friend Cynthia
   · to have Mike pick her up there.
Cynthia's folks live in a new area
    in a new house,
    not as big or nice as Mike's,
    but a lot nicer than ours.
Well, everything went as Carol had planned
    until it was time for Mike to take her home.
Then instead of driving to Cynthia's house,
    he took her right to our house.
Carol said she was so embarrassed
    she burst into tears.
But Mike took her hand
    and gently told her
    that he knew where she lived,
    but that it didn't affect
    how he felt about her.
He said our dad was a respected, hard-working man
    and that his own dad had grown up

in a much simpler home.
He said they'd made a trip back this summer
    to his dad's childhood home.
His grandpa had owned a corner grocery store,
    and the family had lived upstairs.
He said when his dad saw the old place last summer,
    he got so excited.
He got permission to lead the family
    through all the rooms,
    and he told who slept where,
    and he related all the good times they'd had together
    growing up.
Mike said that while listening to his dad
    he began to wonder

107

if maybe his dad hadn't been happier
in that simple upstairs home
than he was now in their gorgeous new home.
By this time Carol had quit crying.
Mike saw her to the door,
    and Carol asked if he'd like to come some night for dinner
    and meet the family.
He said that would be great.
Now I'm excited.
I'll get to meet him
    and see if he's as great as Carol thinks he is.
And I've promised Mom I will behave
    and not embarrass Carol.
I hope I can keep my promise.
Maybe I'll need a little help from you, God.

Let's Think and Talk

1. Why was Carol ashamed of her house?
2. Have you ever been ashamed of your house or family? If so, why?
3. What is important about a home?
4. Can you name some great people who came from little houses?
5. What features does your home have that make you glad to invite your friends home?
6. What qualities does your family have that make it enjoyable for your friends to be in your home?
7. Are there some things you wish were different? What could be done to change them?

Verses to Remember

"Better is a little with the fear of the Lord, than great treasure and turmoil with it. Better is a dish of vegetables where love is, than a fattened ox and hatred with it" (Prov. 15:16, 17, NASB).

39

There Was No Guardrail

Cari's dead.
Cari was only thirteen, Lord—
   too young to die.
She'd still be alive
   if Richard hadn't been drinking and driving.
It was raining hard,
   and the windshield wiper wasn't working right,
   and Richard couldn't see.
The electricity had gone off,
   and there were no streetlights,
   and no guardrail,
   and Richard had been drinking too much.
He drove right into the harbor.
Somehow he got out,
   but Cari never did.
I feel so sad, Lord.
Just kind of numb.
Our teacher told us that
   fourteen teenagers die *every day*
   in drunk-driving accidents
   and 130,000 are injured every year.
Before, those were only figures to me, Lord.
But since Cari died
   the figures have become faces,
   and I find myself getting angry
   listening to beer and wine commercials
   or seeing their ads.
Why do celebrities appear in those ads?
Don't they care about all the kids that die?
Why do the ads pretend alcohol is as wholesome
   as milk,
   or picture drinking as the way to success?

"Life without alcohol
    is like a bird without wings,"
    one of the kids at school said to me.
    "It's the best way to fly."
I don't believe it anymore.
Flying for Richard
    meant drowning for Cari.
It's not fair!

Let's Think and Talk

1. What does alcohol do to one's vision? One's thinking? One's judgment? One's coordination?
2. How much alcohol will make a person drunk?
3. How does regular drinking affect the body?
4. How common is drinking in your school?
5. Why do the kids drink?
6. Where do they get their drinks?
7. Why is it especially serious for *kids* to drink?
8. Why did Susan think it was wrong for celebrities to appear in the ads advertising drinking?
9. If you don't drink, do other kids try to make you feel like dirt? How do you handle this?

Verses to Remember

"Do not get drunk with wine, for that is dissipation, but be filled with the Spirit" (Eph. 5:18, NASB).

"Let us behave properly as in the day, not in carousing and drunkenness, not in sexual promiscuity and sensuality, not in strife and jealousy. But put on the Lord Jesus Christ, and make no provision for the flesh in regard to its lusts" (Rom. 13:13, 14, NASB).

40

Jerry's Van Got Totaled

Dad says Jerry got what he deserved.
Jerry's the guy Tom brought home.
Tom brought him home
    because Jerry's parents had kicked him out of their home.
They'd told him to get a job
    and take care of himself
    because he's twenty-five,
    and anyone twenty-five shouldn't be living off his parents.
But Jerry doesn't have any skills.
He finally found a job at McDonald's,
    but minimum wage wasn't enough to both rent an
    apartment and buy food and gas,
    so Jerry's been living in his van,
    sleeping in it on different parking lots.
Tom finally coaxed Mom and Dad
    to let Jerry stay here for a while
    till he got straightened out.
But he's not straightening out.
He drinks,
    and Dad thinks Jerry stopped maturing when he starting
    drinking.
Jerry says he's been drinking since he was fourteen—
    started with beer.
He boasts how he'd hold his breath
    and the other fellows would pour it down his throat
    straight into his stomach
    using a funnel.
He said it was tricky.
You couldn't breathe
    or you'd choke.
He said he practiced

till he could hold his breath
longer than any of them.
If what Dad thinks is true,
    that Jerry stopped maturing
    when he started drinking,
    then Jerry's fourteen on the inside,
    even if he's twenty-five years old.
Well, you know what happened last night?
Jerry was out with his friends.
He was drunk again
    and started to play around with one of the girls.
She got mad
    and jumped in her car
    and rammed Jerry's van.
It was totaled!
Lots of people saw it happen,
    but only one would give his name as a witness.
The insurance man won't call it an accident,
    so the only thing Jerry can do
    is take the girl to court.
But Jerry's got only one witness,
    and Jerry was drunk and messing around,
    so what chance would he have of winning the case?
Besides, what's the girl got?
Her car isn't worth much now either.
"Poor Jerry!" Mother said. "He's always in trouble."
"Poor Jerry nothing!" Dad exploded.
    "He blew it—he just blew it.
    He got what he deserved.
    With friends like he has
    and carrying on as he does,
    what else can he expect?"
I wonder what'll happen to Jerry.
My dad's mad enough to kick him out,
    and if he does,
    Jerry won't have even a van to sleep in.

Let's Think and Talk

1. When Jerry was fourteen and drinking, what motivated

him to see how much beer could be poured down his throat? What didn't he understand or believe?

2. Is it true that drinking alcohol can arrest the development of adolescents?

3. If you had been Jerry's parents, what would you have done?

4. Did it help Jerry when Tom's parents took him in?

5. Who or what can help Jerry?

6. If *you* don't think drinking is a good thing to do, why do you think other kids disagree with you? Is it possible that kids say it is okay when they really don't think so?

7. Which statements do you think are true? Discuss them.

a. Kids drink because their parents do.

b. Kids drink because alcohol is cheaper and easier to get than drugs.

c. Kids drink to relieve pressure. They believe the world is coming to an end.

d. Kids drink because their parents think it's okay if they do.

e. Kids drink because their friends pressure them.

f. Kids drink because rock music encourages them.

g. Kids drink because they think if celebrities drink, it must be okay to do so.

h. Kids drink because then they can make people laugh.

j. Kids drink because they can't find other kids who refuse to drink.

8. Looking back at your answers, how can you help kids not to start drinking?

A Verse to Remember

"Wine gives false courage; hard liquor leads to brawls; what fools men are to let it master them" (Prov. 20:1, TLB).

114

41

Myrna's Got an Older Boyfriend

I guess some of us girls have been kinda jealous of Myrna
    and the grown-up boyfriend she's had.
He's a neighbor kid who's a lot older than she is,
    a college drop-out who works when he feels like it
    and fools around on his motorcycle in between.
Myrna's mom has been divorced twice and remarried,
    and her present husband doesn't pay any attention to Myrna,
    except when she doesn't clean the house just right
    or doesn't have meals ready on time,
    or the laundry done.
Otherwise he doesn't care about her.
And her mom?
Well, her mom isn't home much.
She still goes off and spends time with her two ex-husbands.
So Myrna has to make it on her own.
For a long time the only friend she had to comfort her
    was her dog.
But then she began to hang around with Rolf,
    this older neighbor boy.
When her mom wasn't home
    and her stepdad wasn't either,
    she'd sneak over to Rolf's,
    and they'd go motorcycle riding together.
Last night she did it again.
But after they took off,
    she realized Rolf was drunk.
He was weaving all over,
    driving like crazy,
    and she was so scared!

Finally they had to stop for gas,
   and she got off and said,
   "I'm not riding with you anymore,"
   and she ran over to a fast-food place
   next to the filling station.
It was late then,
   and she wasn't sure where she was
   or how to get home,
   but she ordered a Coke and sat down to drink it,
   trying to look casual and unconcerned,
   but really scared inside.
Then a policeman came in
   and bought a hamburger
   and sat down across from her.
He kept looking at her turning her Coke
   'round and 'round with her hand,
Finally he asked,
   "You alone?"
She nodded.
"Need help getting home?"
Boy, was she glad to hear that!
On the way home she told him what had happened.
He wanted to know where her parents were,
   and she told him.
He pounded the steering wheel with his fist
   and muttered something under his breath.
Her mom and stepdad still weren't home,
   so she just crawled into bed;
   but, when she finally fell asleep,
   she had nightmares,
   she told me today.
This morning's paper had a picture of a mangled motorcycle.
It was Rolf's.
He's hurt badly.
His parents aren't much different from Myrna's.
The neighbors have been saying
   that his parents haven't even gone to the hospital
   to see Rolf.
I dunno, Lord,
   but I've sure been doing a lot of thinking today.

Let's Think and Talk

1. What do you think Julie had been thinking about?
2. In what way were Myrna's parents responsible for Myrna's actions?
3. Why is it not a good idea for a young teenager to have a boyfriend much older than she?
4. What are the dangers of driving when drunk?
5. How much beer will make you drunk?
6. Do you have pressure put on you at school to drink? How do you handle it?

Verses to Remember

"He who walks with wise men will be wise, but the companion of fools will suffer harm" (Prov. 13:20, NASB).

"Do not be deceived: 'Bad company corrupts good morals' " (1 Cor. 15:33, NASB).

42

Bill Died

Dear God,
I feel so awfully sad tonight.
Our neighbor, Bill, died.
You know how much Bill meant to me.
Since Dad got his promotion
    he's been gone from home so much.
I've really missed him.
But Bill sort of filled in for Dad,
    even though he was a lot older.
After Bill's wife died,
    he took to talking to me
    when I'd come home from school.
I was so surprised to learn
    that he's a Twins fan, too.
We talked baseball a lot.
One day the Twins came to town,
    and Bill invited me to go to the game with him.
I was sure happy!
It was a real exciting game
    with lots of hits and lots of runs
    and it went into extra innings.
That was just the beginning of our going to games together.
As we got to be friends
    I found out Bill was a Christian, too.
After that I started telling him
    about things that bug me.
I told him how difficult it is to study hard enough
    to please my parents,
    because then the kids tease me.
I told him how much I had wanted to play basketball
    but couldn't make the team
    because I'm so short.

I told him how I miss my dad.
He'd listen, and then say,
    "Well, now, let's pray about it,"
    and after we had prayed,
    he'd put his arm around my shoulder and say,
    "Now don't you go frettin' about it anymore.
    The Lord's going to take care of you just fine now."
I always felt so light and relieved
    after those times with Bill,
    and I wouldn't have to take medicine for my stomach pains
    for days.
But a week ago Bill collapsed when he was mowing the lawn,
    and the paramedics rushed him off to the hospital.
"Heart attack," Mom said that evening.
    "Bill's pretty sick."
I felt awful—crushed and bruised and sore,
    and I had to take some of that medicine for my stomach
    pains.
I was too sad to stay home though,
    so I did what we would have done
    if Bill had been home.
I went to a ball game.
Mickey Hatcher hit a home run into the stands,
    and it came right at me.
I caught it—for Bill.
After the game I ran to the gate
    where all the players walk through
    and waited,
    and when Ken Schrom, who had pitched the whole game for
    the Twins came,
    I sucked a deep breath and said,
    "Please, I got Mickey's home run ball.
    Would you autograph it please?"
The next day I asked Mom
    if I could go to the hospital
    to see Bill.
She went with me.
I couldn't get in
    because he was in intensive care,
    but I gave the ball to the nurse,
    and told her how I got it,

and asked her please to give it to Bill,
and she said she would.
Then this afternoon our pastor called
and asked to talk to me.
He said he'd been to see Bill,
and that Bill had sent his love to me.
I asked him if Bill was going to get better soon,
and he paused
and said,
"I have sad news for you, Tim.
Bill died this morning."
He hesitated, and then he said,
"I thought you'd like to know
that he died
holding the ball
you gave to him."
I'm crying, Jesus.
I feel crushed.

Let's Think and Talk

1. What needs did Bill and Tim have in common?
2. What interests did they have in common?
3. Why did Tim like to be with Bill?
4. How did they show affection for each other?
5. Do you have an older friend?
6. In what ways can an older friend be special?
7. What do young people have to give to older people?
8. Has anyone you loved died? Tell what that experience meant to you.

Verses to Remember

An example we have in the Bible of friendship between an older person and a younger person is that between Apostle Paul and Timothy. In writing to Timothy, Paul said: "Pursue righteousness, godliness, faith, love, perseverance and gentleness" (1 Tim. 6:11, NASB).

"A friend loves at all times" (Prov. 17:17, NASB).

43

Why Can't I Paint My Ceiling the Color I Want to?

I'm having trouble with my parents, Lord.
I wanted to redecorate my room,
    and Mom said I could.

But when I said
   I wanted to paint the ceiling
   dark blue, almost black,
   and then put stars on it,
   so it would look like a night sky,
   Mom balked.
"We'll have to think about *that*," she said.
"Why?" I asked.
"Ceilings are hard to paint," she said,
   "and do you know how hard it is to cover dark paint—how
   many coats it takes?"
"Well, then," I said,
   "let me paint the walls orange and yellow and blue
   in big wavy lines
   that go all around the room."
"I think we'd better think about that, too," Mom said.
Give me a break, Lord!
First Mom tells me I can redecorate my room,
   and then she won't go along with anything I want.
What kind of a promise is that?

Let's Think and Talk

1. Why did Lori's mother object to Lori's suggestions?

2. Knowing how a room will look when we have finished redecorating it is tricky. How could Lori have had help so she could be sure the finished look would be attractive and what she really wanted?

3. The way we decorate our homes can tell others something about us. What would you like your room to say about you?

4. What do you think is the best way to handle decorating a teenager's room? Discuss this.

A Verse to Remember

"But let all things be done properly and in an orderly manner" (1 Cor. 14:40, NASB).

44

Boys, Boys, Boys

Boys, boys, boys.
I wish I could forget about boys, Lord.
They're almost all we talk about.
It's hard even in church to think about you, Lord,
 with all the note-writing,
 and giggling,
 and nudging that goes on in the back rows.
There's this one boy I like, Lord,
 but he doesn't like me.
He sits with this other girl,
 and it makes me feel not wanted
 and lonely
 and sad.
I told my friend,
 and she said,
 "I know. I've had it happen to me, too."
I told Mom
 and she said,
 "He's isn't the only one.
 There are plenty of boys around."
Maybe she's right,
 but it doesn't help me much just now.
It's even hard to study
 when all I can think about
 is this boy I like
 who doesn't like me.
What can I do, Lord?

Let's Think and Talk

 1. Have you had a similar experience?

2. Why is learning to maintain balance in life important?

3. What is the difference between being attracted to a person and loving a person?

4. How old do you think young people should be before they "go steady"? Why?

5. Ask your parents and grandparents how they met each other, how long they dated each other, and how they knew they loved each other.

A Verse to Remember

"*Above all else guard your affections.* For they influence everything else in your life" (Prov. 4:23, TLB).

45

How Do I Say "I Love You"?

I've been reading and thinking this morning, Lord.
Rainy days like this when I can't go out
    are good for reading and thinking.
I was reading the thirteenth chapter of 1 Corinthians
    where the Apostle Paul says,
    "The greatest of these is love."
And I've been thinking
    and wondering how I can say
    "I love you"
    to my family.
I haven't been paying too much attention to them lately,
    but I really do love them:
    Mom, Dad, Peg and Nate.
How do I say "I love you" to them?
I guess I say it to my parents
    by doing things without being asked,
    such as making my bed,
    taking out the trash,
    doing the dishes,
    helping with the cleaning.
How do I say "I love you" to my brother and sister?
    By playing with Nate
    when I have to stay home with him
    because Mom and Dad have gone out for the evening,
    and not grumbling that I would rather be at
    Jennifer's house, even if I would.
    By not teasing Peg,
    or using her makeup,
    or reading her diary,
    or borrowing her things without asking.
How do I say "I love you" to all of them?
    By saying, "I'm sorry"

when I've hurt one of them—that happens,
and saying "I was wrong"
when I was wrong,
and "I love you,"
because I really do.
How do Mom and Dad say "I love you" to me?
By giving me a comfortable home,
good food,
the kind of clothes that makes me one of the kids,
health care, the opportunity to study music,
fun vacations together.
I guess most of the time I take these things for granted.
How else do Mom and Dad say "I love you" to me?
By listening to me,
by giving me advice—I sure need it!—
by encouraging me,
by telling me I can do something
when I'm not sure I can,
by defending me,
by giving me some opportunities to solve problems
and make decisions or choices on my own,
and yes, even by disciplining me,
because then I know they really care.
How do Mom and Dad say "I love you" to me?
Mom tells me, "I love you"—almost every day.
Dad can't seem to get the words out,
but he hugs me,
or pats me on the head,
or gives me a gentle wallop on my seat.
I wish Dad would learn to say "I was wrong,"
because sometimes he is,
and it would make it a lot easier for all of us,
but he hasn't learned that yet.
Help him, Lord.
Are there more ways to say "I love you," Lord?
You sure showed your love when you died for us. Maybe that's
the key: to think of others and care about them.
That's hard, Lord.
Most of the time I forget.
Boys and clothes and being popular,
and getting my schoolwork done—

those things get my attention
most of the time—
except on rainy days like today
when I take time to think.
Help me, Lord, to be more thoughtful
so I'll love more.

Let's Think and Talk

1. What skills (cooking, washing the car) have you learned that help you say "I love you" in practical ways? Skills may be considered wealth.

2. How do you feel when your parents show their affection and love for you?

3. How do you feel when you show someone else you love them?

4. When parents give you an opportunity to make a decision, what are they saying about what they think of you?

5. Why does "I was wrong, please forgive me" tell people that we love them?

Verses to Remember

"We know love by this, that He laid down His life for us; and we ought to lay down our lives for the brethren. . . . Little children, let us not love with word or with tongue, but in deed and truth" (1 John 3:16–18, NASB).

46

Why Can't I Choose What I Want to Be?

I hope Mom will accept it
    when I tell her I don't want to be a doctor.
She's always had such big dreams for me:
    Surgeon
    Famous
    Big house
    Cultured
    Musical
The trouble is I've never wanted to be a doctor—
    or even to be rich.
I'm not good at science,
    and blood makes me sick.
And if I have a comfortable home
    and time to spend with the family
    and enough money to live on
    and some to give away,
    I'll be satisfied.
I want to do something where I could work with wood.
I love to work with wood!
Every chance I've had
    I've been going over to Uncle Fred's.
He has a carpenter bench,
    and he's been teaching me how to make things.
Lately I've been working on something special:
    a chest for Mom for her birthday.
I've kept it a secret.
But yesterday, as I was finishing the chest, I nicked my finger.
No biggie really,
    but Mom saw the bandage

and wanted to know what I'd been doing.
I just laughed and said,
    "You'll find out."
And tonight at her birthday party
    she did.
I carried in the chest
    and set it down in front of her.
She squealed
    and "oo"-ed and "ah"-ed
    and ran her hands over it
    and smelled the camphor wood
    and smiled at the aroma.
Afterward she hugged me and said,
    "I'm so proud of you!
    I think it's wonderful you can make something beautiful
    like this."
I guess that made me feel pretty good.
I gave her a quick kiss and said,
    "I'm glad you like it, Mom.
    I loved making it—especially for you."

Let's Think and Talk

1. What do you enjoy doing?

2. If you have thought of a career you would like to pursue, have you mentioned it to your parents? How do they feel about it?

3. What things are important to consider in choosing a career?

4. Do you believe God is concerned about what you choose to do with your life?

5. If you know what you would like to do, what training will you need?

6. What character qualities will you need to complete further training, regardless of what it is?

7. Do your parents enjoy their work? How did they choose to do what they are doing? Is there something they would rather do? Talk about this.

Verses to Remember

"Trust in the Lord with all your heart, and do not lean on your own understanding. In all your ways acknowledge Him, and He will make your paths straight" (Prov. 3:5, 6, NASB).

47

_____

I Felt Like Staying Home

I thought it was going to be really hard
   not to play football this fall
   after I injured my back swimming.
I felt like trying to forget about football,
   like staying home from all the games.
But my friends coaxed me to come to practice anyway.
"We'll miss you," they said.

"Okay," I said,
    thinking I'd go once.
I cheered and yelled
    and during the rest periods
    I told jokes,
    and we all had some good belly laughs.
When the guys went to shower,
    the coach said,
    "I could use a helper this season, Mike.
    Want to give it a try?"
I don't know what he'll expect of me, Lord,
    but I'm excited.
Football season might turn out to be great after all.

Let's Think and Talk

1. How could Mike have reacted when he couldn't play football?

2. What did he choose to do instead?

3. How did his friends show they valued his friendship more than his athletic skill?

4. What do you think the coach valued in Mike so that he asked Mike to be his helper?

5. When have you been prevented from doing something you wanted to do very much?

6. How did you react?

7. How do you feel about the way you handled the situation? How else could you have handled it?

Verses to Remember

"We have this treasure in earthen vessels, that the surpassing greatness of the power may be of God and not from ourselves; we are afflicted in every way, but not crushed; perplexed, but not despairing; persecuted, but not forsaken; struck down, but not destroyed; always carrying about in the body the dying of Jesus, that the life of Jesus also may be manifested in our body" (2 Cor. 4:7–10, NASB).

"Therefore also we have as our ambition . . . to be pleasing to Him" (2 Cor. 5:9, NASB).

48

I Didn't Mean to—I Just Forgot

I'm in trouble, Lord.
Grandma got sick,
    so Mom and Dad and Kathy went to visit her
    and left me home.
I was supposed to water the plants
    while they were gone.
Mom wrote it all out,
    when I was supposed to water which plants and how much.
The first day I was supposed to do it,
    I remembered.
But then my friend Bob started coming home with me from
    school.
We'd watch TV, and we'd bike and work on our model planes,
    and I forgot all about those plants.
Finally after a whole month, Mom came home.
She exploded: "Look at my plants! They're all dead!"
I looked.
Funny, but I hadn't even noticed them before,
    all droopy and brown and dry.
"I'll get you some new plants," I said.
"Fine," Mom said.
    She began figuring on paper.
"How much do you have in your account?" she asked.
    "It'll take about fifty dollars to replace the plants."
"Fifty dollars!" I yelled.
    "How'll I be able to go to camp
    if I have to pay fifty dollars for plants?"
I couldn't believe it!
Mom was taking my offer seriously.

"Maybe you won't go to camp," Mom said quietly.
I can't believe it, Lord.
Does Mom really mean she expects me
    to replace those plants?

Let's Think and Talk

1. Why did Tom neglect watering the plants?
2. To what did he give priority?
3. If Tom had thought through the consequences of his actions, how would he have acted differently?
4. When have you shirked responsibility for fun? What has been the result?
5. Why do people value faithfulness?
6. When does it become especially important for people to know they can rely on you?

A Verse to Remember

"But the fruit of the Spirit is . . . faithfulness. . ." (Gal. 5:22, NASB).

49

Why Didn't Tim Take _Me_ to the Party?

Dear God,
    I'm lying on my bed tonight
    and I have to talk to you about today.
There's this boy I like—Tim.
Can you understand, God,

what it's like for a girl to like a boy?
Well, I like Tim *very* much.
We used to be good friends,
    but now, all of a sudden,
    Tim has gotten interested in Mary.
We had our Halloween party tonight, Lord.
Tim didn't ask me to go with him,
    so Sharon and I went together,
    and you know what?
Tim was there—with Mary!
I got so depressed
    I wanted to go right home.
But Sharon said, "C'mon, Sandy!
    Tim's not the only boy.
    Let's go talk to some of the others."
She dragged me over,
    and one of the boys said,
    "Hey, Sandy, what's this I hear about you placing first in
    the skating contest?"
I was all embarrassed,
    so I just said,
    "I like to skate. In fact, I love to skate!"
"So do I!" he said.
But then he didn't say anything more,
    so I wandered off.
I saw Kim sitting all by herself, so I walked over to her.
Kim doesn't mix much with the kids any time,
    but tonight she looked so sad
    I couldn't help asking what was the matter.
"Do you know what day this is?" she said.
"Sure," I said. "Halloween."
"No, no," she said.
    "It's the anniversary of the day I left my homeland."
"Oh," I said. And then not knowing what else to say I said,
    "Tell me about it."
"Not in here with all this noise," she said.
    "Outside under the stars."
Dear God,
    I never guessed what Kim had gone through.
    Three weeks of fleeing through the jungle
    with rain every day.
    Swarms of mosquitoes.

Hungry.
Living in constant fear of setting off mines
and being blown to bits.
Her mother didn't make it;
she stepped on one.
I'd never known all this before, Lord.
After a while she grew silent.
"Thank you for telling me, Kim," I said.
reaching over to squeeze her hand.
I was crying silently out there in the dark.
I was glad when I heard my dad call,
"Are you out here, Sandy?
I've come to take you and Sharon home."
"Can we give Kim a ride too?" I asked.
Only after I got home
did I realize
I'd forgotten all about boys
and being jealous
because Tim had taken Mary to the party,
and not me.

Let's Think and Talk

1. How did Sandy show self-control?
2. What helped her get through the evening?
3. What was the result?
4. In her preoccupation with boys, what had Sandy been missing out on?
5. Have you ever liked a boy who doesn't seem to like you? How have you handled the situation?
6. When was the time you were most jealous? How important does it seem to you now?
7. How can you handle feelings of jealousy?

Verses to Remember

"Do not merely look out for your own personal interests, but also for the interests of others" (Phil. 2:4, NASB).

"Let us not become conceited, provoking and envying each other" (Gal. 5:26, NIV).

50

I Got Caught!

Dear God,
I got caught.
In the most incredible way, I got caught!
Jenny and I have been skipping school
    to go to the mall
    and look around,
    and Mom and Dad hadn't found out.
But yesterday the principal called me in
    and gave me a letter to bring home to my dad.
It was sealed,
    but anyone could guess what was in it.
On the way home Jenny and I were talking about what to do.
"Just don't give it to your dad," Jenny said.
    "He'll never know,
    and the principal will think
    your dad doesn't care enough to come and see him about
    your skipping."
I didn't think I dared to do that,
    but after saying good-bye to Jenny at her house,
    I turned the corner
    and there were Mr. Murphy's trash cans
    still sitting out.
I don't know why,
    but all of a sudden
    I just threw the envelope into one of the cans,
    and it landed face down.
Good riddance! I thought,
    and walked on home.
Today when Dad came home from work,
    he called me.
"Missy," he said, "where's the note the principal gave you
    yesterday to give to me?

His secretary called today
and wanted to know what my answer was.
I said I'd call back tomorrow.
Now where's the note, Missy?"
I felt my neck turning red,
and my mouth got all dry.
"Ah, Dad, don't get all worked up," I said.
"I've skipped school once or twice—that's all.
Nothing to get all excited about."
"Oh!" Dad said.
I could tell by the set of his jaw
he'd be going to see the principal for sure.
I felt pretty scared
and escaped outside.
I jumped on my bike to ride over to Jenny's.
Just as I was wheelin' around the corner,
there was old Mr. Murphy raking leaves.
"Oh, Missy," he said,
"wait a minute.
I have something for you."
He went into the house and came out with—I couldn't believe
it!—
the letter.
"Must have blown off when you biked past yesterday," he said.
"Landed right in my trash can."
"Jeepers!" I said. "Thanks. Thanks . . . a lot."
It almost burned in my hand.
"What'll I do now?" I asked Jenny
when I got to her house.
"Well, we might as well open it," Jenny said.
We ripped it open.
It was on school stationery,
and it was a typewritten invitation to my dad to be the
graduation speaker!
"Wow!" I said. "What do we do now?"
"You don't have much choice, do you?" Jenny said,
both giggling and looking scared.
Dad listened to what I had to say.
He read the note and then he cleared his throat.
"Now about this other matter," he began, "maybe we should
talk about

that too—don't you agree, Missy?"
I nodded.
I was still scared,
    but I knew that when he added "Missy,"
    our talk would turn out all right.

Let's Think and Talk

1. Role play the conversation that followed between Missy and her father, only reverse the roles. Ask your father to be Missy and you be Missy's father.

2. Can your parents recall any time they tried to hide something from their parents or employers or from each other? How did it end?

3. Skipping school and then being deceitful may seem like minor offenses, but why are they serious?

4. In the Bible we have a very sad account of what happened when King David skipped out on going to war with this armies and stayed home instead. This act, in turn, led to a deceitful act. You may want to read about it in 2 Samuel 11:1–27 and 12:1–23.

Verses to Remember

"Blessed is the man . . . in whose spirit there is no deceit!" (Ps. 32:2, NASB).

"Who is the man who desires life, and loves length of days that he may see good? Keep your tongue from evil, and your lips from speaking deceit" (Ps. 34:12, 13, NASB).

51

Does Winning Have to Be Everything?

I feel terrible, Lord.
Our teams were tied up
    in the last half of the tenth inning.
I was catcher for our baseball team,
    and their left fielder was on second.
I fumbled the pitcher's next throw,
    and the fellow on second slid into third.
That was bad enough,
    but when I threw the next ball to the pitcher, it went wild,
    and the fellow on third got home,
    so the other team won the game.
All the guys on our team yelled and screamed at me.
Our coach was jumping up and down.
"Defeat is worse than death!" he fumed,
    and he was so, so mad.
I felt like the smallest, ugliest worm you could ever find.
I got away as fast as I could.
But I feel awful.
How will I ever go back?
What will happen if I blunder again?

Let's Think and Talk

1. Why did Ron feel he was a failure?
2. What attitude is most common in sports, both amateur and professional?
3. If a person feels he or she always has to win, what is apt to happen to that person? How will that person be tempted to play?

4. Here are comments by two coaches. Discuss them.

"Winning isn't everything; it's the *only* thing" (Vince Lombardi, former Green Bay Packers coach).

"The chase is more important than the winning. I don't think I'd enjoy it as much if I knew I would always be a winner" (Tom Landry, Dallas Cowboys coach).

Verses to Remember

"I cry aloud to God, aloud to God, that he may hear me. In the day of my trouble I seek the Lord" (Ps. 77:1, 2, RSV).

"Who, O God, is like you? Though you have made me see troubles, many and bitter, you will restore my life again; from the depths of the earth you will again bring me up. You will increase my honor and comfort me once again" (Ps. 71:20, 21, NIV).

52

I Couldn't Find the Right Valentine

Dear God,
>Thank you for parents who understand
>when I mean to do well,
>but botch things up.

Today was Valentine's Day.

I wanted so badly to find the perfect valentine for Mom and
Dad,
>because I love them so much.

I had been looking for days,
>but hadn't found the right one,
>so I was getting desperate.

I had only a couple hours after school,
>and then we were going to have early basketball practice.

I looked and looked and finally found one that read:

>"This comes to warmly thank you for your patience and advice,
>Your thoughtful understanding, your help and sacrifice.
>It brings so many memories too special to forget,
>Of the love you've always given, the example that you've set.
>It comes to wish you happiness today and always too,
>And it brings a world of deepest love and gratitude to you."

It was expensive,
>but I had to get it.

After I paid for it,
>I glanced at my watch.

Oh, oh! Barely time to run home with the card,
>and then I'd have to scramble to get to practice on time.

When I walked into the house,
>I smelled beef roast and homemade rolls.

Mom and Dad and Sheila were sitting at the dining room table.

Mom had decorated the room with hearts and streamers.

"We waited and waited for you," Mom said.

"I knew you had practice,
   so I planned an early dinner.
Dad came home early,
   so we could eat together."
"I'm sorry," I stammered.
"Never mind," Dad said, "sit down now and dig in."
"I can't," I stammered. "I have to get to practice."
"And not eat?" Mom said.
   There was a heavy silence.
   "I even baked your favorite chocolate cake," she said.
I was feeling like dirt,
   but I pulled out the card I had been holding behind my back.
"I'm sorry," I said. "I really am.
   You know how much I like beef roast and chocolate cake,
   and how much I appreciate all the work you went to. But I
   couldn't find the right card until just a few minutes ago.
   I've been looking and looking."
Mom took the card and read it
   and then handed it to Dad.
"I'll put a plate for you in the fridge," she said.
   "You can warm it in the microwave when you come home."
Dad had read the card,
   and he had that funny look on his face that he gets when
   he's trying not to cry.
Mom's eyes were wet.
She came over and hugged me and said,
   "Have a good practice, Son.
   We love you.
   The card is beautiful,
   but you are even more beautiful."
When I came home from practice
   Mom was already in bed.
I tiptoed into her room.
She was asleep,
   but the card I had given Mom and Dad
   was already framed and hanging on their wall.

Let's Think and Talk

1. How do we know there was a good relationship between
Ron and his parents?

2. How did Ron want to express his love?

3. How did his parents want to express their love?

4. What did Ron's parents say and do to make him feel better?

5. When we love people, why is it important to express our love in words and actions?

A Verse to Remember

"Beloved, let us love one another, for love is from God; and everyone who loves is born of God and knows God" (1 John 4:7, NASB).

53

The New Kid

You were good to me today, Lord,
    and I thank you.
I have been so lonely since leaving my own country
    and coming here to the big United States.
It's been hard.
I've studied hard to learn English,
    but there still are many words I do not know.
I do well in math,
    because numbers are the same in all languages.
    But I have difficulty with the other subjects.
My body isn't strong enough yet for me
    to be really good at sports,
    and my classmates laugh at my clothes.
They say if you don't wear "preppy clothes,"
    you're not "in."
I don't know what "preppy" means,
    but I understand very well what it means
    not to be "in."
It hurts not to be "in."
Sometimes I get angry thinking about it.
I have trouble with the food too, Lord.
    I don't like hamburgers.
    Do I have to like hamburgers to be "in"?
I like to sleep on the floor.
    The kids think that is weird.
    Why is that weird, Lord?
    What's wrong with sleeping on the floor?
Well, all these things make me different
    from most of the kids,
    and so school hasn't been easy.
But today you were good to me, Lord.
Our class was learning how TV programs are prepared.
They were choosing someone to interview,

and one of the boys said,
  "I nominate Cheng. He can tell us about his country."
I was so surprised.
I wondered if they were thinking
  they would get some good laughs
  out of my English.

But I was so happy to talk about my country
    that the words just flowed.
Afterward many of them came
    and said my country sounded like a beautiful place,
    and they hoped they could visit it someday.
One of the fellows said
    they needed a scorekeeper for their baseball games.
    Could I help them?
And another fellow asked
    if I could come home with him some night for dinner so I
    could tell his family what I had told the class.
Tonight I don't feel as lonely as I usually do, Lord.
I feel as if maybe I do belong, and maybe this country is my
    country, too.

Let's Think and Talk

1. Do you have any students from other countries in your school, church or neighborhood?

2. Have you become acquainted with them?

3. How is your style of life different from theirs?

4. Have you ever eaten their food? Have you ever invited them to your home for a meal?

5. Have you ever had the experience of not feeling "in"? Tell about it. What helped?

6. Have your parents or teachers ever felt they didn't belong? How did they handle the situation?

7. Why is it a mistake to not accept people because their dress or customs and culture is different from ours?

8. What is necessary in your school in order to be part of the "in" crowd? How do you feel about this?

Verses to Remember

"Do not mistreat or do violence to the stranger" (Jer. 22:3, NASB).

"Do not neglect to show hospitality to strangers, for by this some have entertained angels without knowing it" (Heb. 13:2, NASB).

54

Zap 'Em

I've lost my friend, Lord.
Michael and I used to do so many things together:
    baseball and tennis,
    shooting baskets,
    fishing and swimming,
    playing chess,
    and building model planes.
Now all Michael wants to do is play video games:
    Donkey Kong,
    Asteroids,
    Space Invaders,
    King Gorilla,
    Frogger.
I think Michael has played them all.
He thinks nothing of shooting ten dollars
    in an afternoon.
He jumps up and down and yells
    when he can "kill" 12 million space invaders.
He throws a tantrum when he is "eaten,"
    and he gets so depressed
    he won't talk to anyone,
    not even me.
I used to play the games with him,
    and I liked the challenge
    of having to think through a problem,
    but after a while it grew old for me.
I don't like getting so excited all the time.
It leaves me with headaches.
And I'd rather talk with friends
    and hear their voices.
Besides, I don't feel really good
    "zapping enemies" all the time.

Michael can't understand why I feel this way,
and sometimes when all the kids want to play,
I don't know what to do.
Sometimes I play for a while,
and then drift away quietly.
Sometimes I suggest a ball game instead.
Sometimes the kids go along with me;
sometimes they don't.
Dear Lord, can you understand
how growing up in a computer age is different?
At least that's what my folks say,
but I'm not sure they really understand what it's like
for me.

Let's Think and Talk

1. What positive effects do video games have on people who use them?

2. What negative effects may they have on those who play them?

3. What do video games and the amount of time we spend playing them tell us about what we value?

4. What would be some good guidelines to draw up for playing the games? How much time should be spent playing? How much money?

5. If a person has become addicted to the games, what can be done to break the addiction?

6. What other things besides playing video games can one do that will also sharpen one's ability to think and plan?

7. Should games be valued most for what they teach us or for the enjoyment and relaxation they give us?

A Verse to Remember

"Try to learn what is pleasing to the Lord" (Eph. 5:10, RSV).

55

Sometimes Kids Get Caught in the Middle

Dear God,
I've been playing cover-up with my friends
  and family,
    giggling and acting silly,
    when all the time, inside,
    I've been hurting really badly.
I haven't wanted to believe, Lord,
    that it's happening in *our* family,
    that Mom and Dad are talking about divorce.
I can't believe it.
I don't *want* to believe it!
I'm mad!
Don't they care about kids?
Don't they think about what this will do to us?
I feel all knotted up inside.
I wish I could cry,
    but I can't,
    so instead I act dumb
    and try to get others to laugh,
    but it's not really the way I feel way deep down inside, Lord.
I hurt.
I hurt worse than I ever knew I could hurt.
Can you help me?

Let's Think and Talk

1. What do you think are some of the things Debbie is afraid will happen if her mother and father divorce?

2. Instead of trying to pretend that these things aren't really

happening, what would be better for Debbie to do?

3. What possible solutions could there be for the things Debbie fears? Talk about the solutions, one at a time.

4. How can Debbie be helped to continue to love and respect both her parents?

5. Who do you think would be able to help Debbie?

6. Why do parents break up?

7. What good things can come out of the tragedy of a divorce?

8. In what ways can different members of a family have different feelings about a divorce?

Verses to Remember

"He [God] Himself has said, 'I will never desert you, nor will I ever forsake you,' so that we confidently say, 'The Lord is my helper, I will not be afraid. What shall man do to me?' " (Heb. 13:5, 6, NASB).

56

Cults

I never thought it would happen to someone I knew,
    but it has.
Randy's oldest brother, John, has joined a cult.
Randy said his mom and dad were so shook up last night
    when they discovered
    Randy had moved out
    that they were like chickens caught on a freeway
    with cars speeding past.
His mom cried and screamed, he said.
His dad pounded the walls and the table with his fists
    and paced back and forth.
Randy said three young people
    dressed in long yellow robes
    had been standing on the sidewalk
    across from John's high school
    day after day,
    waiting to talk to anyone who would listen.
John's always been the kind to talk to anyone,
    so he stopped to listen
    and ask questions.
I don't know exactly what happened next,
    except I guess one day
    John went home with them.
Randy said after that John really began to change.
He used to joke and kid a lot,
    but he became really serious.
He spent a lot of time away from home,
    and when he was home,
    he didn't talk much with the family but went up to his room
    and shut the door.
When his mom and dad tried to ask questions,
    he wouldn't answer,

but just walked away.
Randy said he tried one day,
    and John just said,
    "Shut up! You don't know anything.
    Nobody in this house does."
Randy feels terrible,
    and so do his mom and dad.
Help them, Lord Jesus, and show them what to do.

Let's Think and Talk

1. Have you seen or talked to anyone who belongs to a cult? Which cult?

2. How much should you let other people tell you what to do or not do?

3. Is it right to try to change the beliefs of others? Discuss this.

4. What are some of the characteristics of cults?

5. Someday you may be approached by some cult followers to join their group. What questions will be wise for you to ask? What precautions will you want to take?

A Verse to Remember

"Dear friends, do not believe every spirit, but test the spirits to see whether they are from God, because many false prophets have gone out into the world" (1 John 4:1, NIV).

57

Playing Fair in Sports

I didn't know what it would be like
    playing on the school football team.
"Winning is the *only* thing!" our coach yells at us
    over and over.
"We've *got* to succeed.
    We've *got* to be the number one team.
    We've *got* to win.
Win, win, win! Think 'win!' all the time."
It seems like
    if we have to trip someone to win,
    we trip.
If we have to play dirty to win,
    we play dirty.
If we hurt ourselves,
    we keep on playing,
    no matter how much it hurts.
It seems that getting mad at the other team
    and hating their guts
    and going all out to slaughter them
    is what we're expected to do
    if doing it
    will mean winning.
I feel kind of sick about it all.
Winning isn't everything to me.
In fact, winning all of the time
    would take the fun out of winning
    when we do,
    wouldn't it?
And who can be first all of the time anyway?
Don't we have to learn to lose, too?
Isn't it better to play fair
    and not cheat
    or break the rules,

than it is to play crooked
and lose?
I feel all depressed, Lord.
Will you show me what to do?

Let's Think and Talk

1. Discuss these two statements:

"Winning is living. Every time you win, you're reborn. When you lose, you die a little" (George Allen, pro football coach).

"There are many victories worse than a defeat. Any coward can fight a battle when he's sure of winning; but give me the person who has pluck to fight when he's sure of losing" (George Eliot, author).

2. How would you define winning?

3. What values are sacrificed when getting the highest score is the one and only objective?

4. How are winners in the sports world rewarded? How does this affect players in regard to how they play the games?

A Verse to Remember

"I strive always to keep my conscience clear before God and man" (Acts 24:16, NIV).

58

I Hadn't Known How Rich Grandpa Was

Yesterday was Grandpa's funeral.
I had thought it would be an awful day
    with lots of crying
    and everybody real sad,
    but it wasn't.
Of course, it was a funny feeling
    thinking I'd never see Grandpa again,
    or go on walks with him,
    or be able to talk with him anymore,
    but when I listened to what people said about Grandpa,
    I felt so proud he was my Grandpa.
"He towed my car home once when it broke down,"
    one of Grandpa's neighbors said.
"He came and repaired my garage door when it broke,"
    a widow said.
"He used to bring us fresh popcorn," some old people said who
    live in an extended care home.
"He took my boys to ball games when I was gone from home on
    business,"
    one of the men at church said.
"One year I was out of work for months. Fritz gave me a loan
    and didn't charge interest," an engineer said.
Listening to all the people,
    I decided that though I hadn't realized it before, Grandpa
    really was a very rich man,
    even though he never lived in a big, fancy house
    or drove an expensive car.
He was rich in friends.
I hope mine will be a happy funeral like Grandpa's, God.

Let's Think and Talk

1. When you go to a funeral, what do you often learn about the person who has died that you didn't know before? If you haven't been to a funeral, ask your parents or some other adults this question.

2. What do people remember about persons who have died?

3. What would you like people to remember about you when you die? Write the kind of obituary you would like to have read at your funeral.

Verses to Remember

"Command those who are rich in this present world not to be arrogant nor to put their hope in wealth, which is so uncertain, but to put their hope in God, who richly provides us with everything for our enjoyment. Command them to do good, to be rich in good deeds, and to be generous and willing to share" (1 Tim. 6:17, 18, NIV).